MINORITY COMMUNITY LANGUAGES IN SCHOOL

National Congress on Languages in Education

Minority community languages in school

NCLE Papers and Reports 4

The first of two volumes from Working Parties
for the Third Assembly, Nottingham 1982

Edited by Euan Reid

Centre for Information on Language Teaching and Research

First published 1984

Copyright © 1984 Centre for Information on Language Teaching
and Research
ISBN 0 903466 70 8

Printed in Great Britain by Multiplex Techniques Ltd

Published by Centre for Information on Language Teaching and
Research, Regent's College, Inner Circle, Regent's Park, London
NW1 4NS

CONTENTS

APPENDICES   Page

INTRODUCTION

Euan Reid

This Working Party was set up in November 1980, following a resolution put forward at the July 1980 Assembly of the National Congress on Languages in Education by representatives of the Co-Ordinating Committee (now National Council) for Mother Tongue Teaching, the National Association for Multiracial Education, and the National Association of Teachers of English, as follows:

> 'Since linguistic variety is a resource to be valued by a multi-cultural society, steps should be taken to maintain, develop and build upon languages and varieties in use by all ethnic groups resident in the United Kingdom.'

This resolution also received widespread support from other constituent organisations present at Durham, including teachers of Italian and Dutch, and the welcome can probably be explained in terms of the growing acceptance by language educators in Britain that 'something needed to be done' in this field, combined with an uncertainty about precisely what that something was and how it was to be achieved.

So, on the basis of the 1980 Assembly resolution, the task assigned to the Working Party was:

> 'To examine the implications for schools and LEAs of the range of languages at present in use among members of ethnic and cultural minorities'.

> and

> 'To make recommendations for more effective development and exploitation of these language resources for the benefit of the pupils and of the wider community'.

The membership of the Working Party was as follows:

John Broadbent (Modern Languages Department, Alperton High School, Brent)
Barré Fitzpatrick (Education Department, Bradford College)
June Geach (Centre for Information on Language Teaching and Research)
M Akram Khan-Cheema (Education Department, Bradford Metropolitan Borough Council (formerly Birmingham MBC))
Rosamond Mitchell (Education Department, University of Stirling
Otto Polling, (Thomas Gray Centre, Slough)

Euan Reid (Linguistic Minorities Project, University of London
                    Institute of Education), Chair
Arturo Tosi (Department of Modern Languages, Oxford Polytechnic)
Roy Truman (National Council for Mother Tongue Teaching), Secretary
John Wright (Advisory Centre for Education (formerly ILEA's World in
                    a City Project))
John Singh (HMI), observer

The Working Party had its first planning meeting in December 1980, three further one-day meetings in March, June and September 1981 at which it discussed papers produced and circulated by members between meetings, a two-day meeting in November 1981 at which the contents of the Working Party Report, included as Section A of this collection, were agreed, and a meeting in January 1982 to agree textual revisions. Several further meetings followed in the spring of 1982, to discuss the revision of the papers contributed for circulation to NCLE constituent organisations and participants in the 1982 Assembly (included in substantially unrevised form as Section B of this collection); to launch the exercise described by John Wright in Section C under the title of the poster he designed - 'Growing up bilingual' and to prepare for the Working Party's participation in the Assembly. Rather belatedly, we also commissioned one or two accounts of interesting practice: only the description of the teaching of Gujarati in Brent was received early enough to table at the Assembly in Nottingham, along with a preliminary report on 'Growing up bilingual'.

The Report and other papers circulated in the early months of 1982 and presented in Nottingham in July were received with interest, and with a general willingness to concede the importance of the issues raised and the persuasiveness of many of the principles and proposals put forward. This welcome was accompanied, however, by a certain scepticism about the practicalities of implementation and some anxiety about the effects of what some saw as further pressure on scarce and hard-pressed resources for the language curriculum. The response of the National Association of Language Advisers to the Working Party's Report concluded, for example:

'The document is a demanding, searching one which has support from NALA. It does come at a time when resources are scarce. One cannot see it being implemented in its present form very soon. However, acceptance of a community comes only with acceptance of the value and importance of its language. If we are to be a multi-cultural society, we must be a multi-lingual one, whilst accepting that English will always be the unifying and dominant language for us all.'

Several developments have taken place since July 1982 in areas discussed by the Working Party which readers of these papers may be interested in following up. The Schools Council Mother-Tongue

Project has made great progress in the production and piloting of its teaching materials in Bengali and in Modern Greek, as well as in those designed to encourage awareness of and hospitality to bilingualism among monolingual teachers and pupils. (The contact address is in Appendix II.) With reference to the evolution of more appropriate public examinations in minority languages, the Schools Council had also made progress by the end of 1982 by commissioning reports and proposals for new exams in Hindi, Urdu and Modern Greek. It remains to be seen whether their successors in the Secondary Examinations Council will accept the general thrust of the suggestions put forward. On in-service teacher training, the Royal Society of Arts Examinations Board has agreed to the launching of a pilot scheme for a Certificate in the Teaching of Community Languages, beginning in 1983. (Further information may be obtained from the RSA, 8 John Adam Street, London WC2.)An important Report has appeared, of a study undertaken for the Swann Committee, by Professor Maurice Gaft and Dr. Madeleine Atkins: <u>Training teachers of ethnic minority community languages</u>. Finally, several LEAs have adopted more systematic and explicit policies, notably ILEA, Nottinghamshire and Bradford, whose policy document on 'Community Language Teaching' draws very heavily on the NCLE Working Party's recommendations.

The Working Party members, then, have good reason to feel heartened by progress so far. I should like on their behalf to thank the Swann Commmittee of Enquiry into the Education of Children from Ethnic Minority Groups for the financial support which made the completion of the Report and Papers possible. Two members of the Working Party whose names do not appear against particular contributions to this publication deserve a special mention: Rosamond Mitchell, who provided the first, crucial drafts of the 'rationale' section of the Report and of the summary discussion document which now forms Appendix III, and Roy Truman, our Secretary, who gave us the very great benefit of his wide experience of language education and of multicultural education, while maintaining unconvincingly to the very end his lack of specialist knowledge in our field.

Euan Reid
Working Party Chairman   July 1983

Section A: The Working Party Report

EDUCATIONAL CONTEXT

The 1944 Education Act for England and Wales requires Local Education Authorities

'to contribute towards the spiritual, moral, mental and physical development of the community by securing that efficient education ... shall be available to meet the needs of the population of their area'

and further requires the provision of

'such varieties of instruction and training as may be desirable in view of... different ages, abilities and aptitudes....'

These widely accepted principles have so far been interpreted with reference to the new linguistic minorities in Britain almost entirely in terms of support for the teaching of English as a second language. Substantial support for ESL will continue to be needed, to ensure effective access to equality of economic and social opportunity. However, we would suggest that where 'the population of their area' includes a significant proportion of speakers and potential speakers of languages other than English, LEAs ought also to consider responding more fully than most have so far felt able to particular linguistic 'abilities and aptitudes' among their populations.

We believe that there are possibilities at various points within the education service for meeting the wishes of many parents and community organisations for some encouragement of people's natural interest in the living languages of their communities, and we set out the case for various types of initiative at school level in the first section of our Report.

We see it as desirable too that some of the languages we are concerned with might be made more widely available to people who have no direct personal or family connections with the languages. This part of our argument we would want to relate to the general justifications which are offered for studying languages, usefully summarised in a recent booklet from the <u>National Association of Language Advisers</u> (NALA, n.d. 2.2). By learning another language in school it is suggested that 'Pupils may be equipped...to operate in a range of defined situations among speakers of the language studied' and that this might provide '...for those who discontinue language learning while at school, a basis for a return to language learning later in life, whether in connection with work or leisure.' Language learning is also claimed to 'encourage verbal awareness' and '...promote the ability to understand the working of language by looking at it from

1

outside.' Furthermore, '...the skills of analysis, classification and reference; the making of analogies, and the drawing of inferences' are developed. The 'cultural' justification is expressed in terms of '...the urgent need to encourage cultural adaptability in an increasingly multiracial society, and in a world where travel abroad, whether for business or pleasure, is a common experience for millions.' NALA also points (1.1.5., op cit) to the 'increasing diversity of languages used as mother tongue by linguistic minorities in the UK' and suggests that 'It is not unreasonable to think that the school curriculum should take account of this picture.' Proposition 9 in HMI's View of the Curriculum (DES 1980) also refers to the need to reconsider modern language policy in this context: 'There is also a strong case for a modern language in the education of all pupils, and for the establishment of national policy on the place of individual languages in the system. Account has also to be taken of the presence in many schools of British-born pupils from ethnic minority groups who are already acquainted with languages other than English, and the children of migrants from EEC and other European countries, who wish to maintain and develop their mother tongues.'

We urge readers to consider then whether, for some learners in some circumstances, the general educational aims implicit in the justifications just rehearsed might not be at least as satisfactorily achieved through the study of one of the languages of a minority community in Britain, as through one of the more traditionally taught languages. (There is some danger in this suggestion that ethnic minority pupils might be deprived of access to the study of the traditional school languages: we believe this to be undesirable, and that the way to avoid it is to support the general provision of at least two languages in addition to English for most pupils.)

It is encouraging to find positive references of the kind NALA and the HMIs make to minority community languages in schools, but we are well aware that the practical and logistical problems of turning goodwill into good practice are very considerable. We have not attempted in what follows to offer answers to all the questions that will certainly occur to readers. Nor do we pretend that it will be possible in any future resource situation that seems plausible at the moment for every school to offer, even to every pupil with family connections with a particular language, the option of studying that language on the school premises and in school time. Our Working Party Report and the related papers are intended simply as contributions to thinking about how even quite a modest increase in support for such languages might help, to borrow the words of the final aim in the draft national criteria for foreign languages at 16+:

> 'to encourage an unprejudiced approach to other cultures and civilisations, thereby contributing to the formation of a more tolerant society.'

A RATIONALE FOR MINORITY LANGUAGES IN EDUCATION

The issue of minority languages in education is not a new one for British society. After centuries of discouragement and even oppression, the indigenous minority languages of Britain, Welsh and Gaelic, have won places for themselves within the mainstream school systems of Wales and Scotland, and are taught at primary and secondary levels both to children whose main home languages are Welsh or Gaelic, and to those whose home language is English. In addition, both these languages are used to some extent as the medium of instruction in bilingual programmes. However, these cases apart, Britain has until recently scarcely attempted to respond to diverse linguistic backgrounds in its school population. The emergence of many new minority language communities using a wide range of European and Asian languages has, broadly speaking, been met by an expectation of eventual linguistic assimilation. Within the educational system, effectively the only linguistic adaptation made to the appearance of large numbers of children speaking languages other than English has been the provision of some teaching of English as a second language, seen as a preliminary to full integration into English-medium schooling. The only language element in the curriculum apart from English is likely to be the study of one or two European languages chosen from a small range which reflects a rather limited view of Britain's present cultural and political needs.

The inadequacy of the traditional British ethnocentric curriculum for a now multi-racial and multi-cultural society has in recent years been increasingly remarked on. The curricular debate has not yet, however, led to any substantial increase in support for minority languages in education. As the Schools Council report, Multi-ethnic education: the way forward (Little and Willey, 1981), makes clear, the teaching of the newer minority languages within mainstream schooling is very rare, while their use as a medium of instruction is non-existent, at least at secondary school level. The cautious DES response even to the limited proposals of the July 1977 Directive of the Council of the European Community on the education of the children of migrant workers (DES, 1981), and the small number of research and development projects being sponsored by the DES and EC in this area reflect the fact that the issue of minority languages in education remains marginal, even in the consciousness of professional educationists concerned with language.

The United Kingdom has thus been slow to follow the example of several developed countries in making available minority languages as a normal element in mainstream schooling, at least for those children to whom a minority language is a home language. In Sweden, for example, although it is important not to idealise the situation there, parents now have a legal right within certain generously drawn limits to ask for instruction in the home language within

3

normal school hours. This right has been exercised for more than half of the eligible children, and instruction is currently being provided in over 50 languages, in a variety of organisational modes for different age levels (Ekstrand, 1980). Canada (Cummins, 1981) and Australia (Garner, 1981) are among other countries which are developing their provision of minority language education in a substantial way.

By comparison with the indigenous minority language communities, which have developed effective pressure groups to lobby for state support for the teaching of Welsh and Gaelic, the newer minority language communities of Britain have not so far had significant success in seeking minority language teaching within the school system. That demand for such teaching does exist emerges from the previously mentioned Schools Council report. This provides evidence for a substantial level of requests to local authorities for minority language instruction in schools, at least in areas with large minority language groups. (It also reports a wish on the part of the language teaching profession in such areas to respond to this demand, which is however being frustrated by lack of resources and trained personnel.) Other very telling evidence for the existence of community support for minority language teaching consists in the large-scale development of voluntary mother tongue schools outside the mainstream school system (Saifullah Khan, 1978).

It is properly part of NCLE's role to respond to this interest, to investigate different possibilities for minority language education and to make proposals for its development within the mainstream, educational system. A well thought out minority language programme in schools could benefit individual children (minority and majority) the minority language communities as a whole, and the wider society. As the general debate continues on the multi-cultural curriculum, we believe that NCLE should ensure that the linguistic aspects are taken fully into account.

Types of minority language education

Many different patterns of minority language education have been discussed in the research literature, and those best suited to particular contexts are a matter for empirical investigation within these settings. However, four broad types of initiative appear to us to merit priority consideration in developing minority language education policies for mainstream schools in Britain in the 1980s. These are:

(1) Minority languages in school reception.

(2) Minority language development, including literacy.

(3) Minority language learning for monolingual English-speaking children.

(4) Minority language as medium of instruction.

Note: L1 = first language; L2 = second language

(1) Minority languages in school reception

The child starting school is taking a huge step even when the languages of home and school are very closely related. Where the languages are quite obviously different a gulf exists between home and school which may work against settling easily into school, and against subsequent performance there. The negative evaluation of the home implicit in the widespread discouragement from using the mother tongue for any purpose whatsoever at school seems at the least unlikely to foster self-confidence, or relations with teacher or classmates based on mutual respect.

Current research on early language development also suggests that the quality of linguistic interaction between adults and children in the early years is an important element in the subsequent development of literacy skills and of the ability to use language in the 'context-reduced' situations crucial for academic success (see, for example, Wells, 1979 and 1981, quoted in Swain, 1981). It is, of course, not possible for monolingual English-speaking teachers to build on or extend the existing communicative ability of minority L1 children in this pre-literacy stage. The case, therefore, in favour, of providing minority L1 children entering pre-school and first school with bilingual teachers and assistants capable of interacting freely with them, responding to what they say and relating instruction to their interests and existing linguistic abilities as well as developing their new ones, appears to us to be a very strong one, whatever decisions are taken regarding the place of the various languages in later education. Clearly schools with a particularly diverse linguistic composition could not expect to provide equally satisfactorily in this respect for all their pupils: this is not, in our view, a good reason for not developing initiatives of this kind wherever circumstances do allow.

In many countries programmes of pre-school and early primary education exist for minority L1 children, taught partly or wholly through the medium of minority language by teachers competent in it (see for example Cummins, 1981). This is found useful even where children move subsequently to majority-language-medium education, as is the case, for example, in many American programmes for minority language groups. The positive experience of those schools which took part in the Mother-Tongue and English Teaching Project in Bradford (MOTET, 1981) lends general support to the carefully planned use of minority languages in school reception in appropriate areas. (This Project involved teaching the normal infant curriculum partly through English, partly through Panjabi.) Initial school reception making use of the minority language is, of course, also a logical first step for children moving on to programmes aiming to consolidate and attend their bilingual competence in the mother tongue and in English.

(2) Minority language development, including literacy

A crucial question in the area of minority language education concerns the development of minority language literacy skills by minority L1 children. It appears to be a virtually unquestioned assumption at present that, in order for these children to succeed in English medium education, the development of literacy skills in English must be fully established first, with minority language literacy being developed only much later, if at all, and by some agency other than the 'ordinary' school. Instruction in mother tongue literacy skills is consequently still very rare in British schools, although the work of the Schools Council Mother-Tongue Project, which began in 1981, is likely to extend it significantly, in the first place with particular reference to Greek and Bengali (see Appendix for more details). While such instruction is an important part of the programme of community language schools, a considerable proportion (perhaps even a majority) of minority language-speaking children appear in present circumstances not to have the opportunity of developing functional literacy in their mother tongue.

The assumption that the current development of minority language literacy would be harmful to the development of literacy in English appears to be groundless, at least as far as experience elsewhere can suggest. In fact, in some contexts it seems that the development of minority language literacy skills has had generally beneficial educational effects, including better subsequent performance in the majority language (see review by Lambert, 1977; also Rosier and Farella, 1976). Even where such enhancement has not been demonstrated, it has been shown that minority L1 literacy teaching can at least be included in the primary school programme with no adverse effects on majority language skills (see, for example, Cohen, 1975).

Furthermore, the development of mother-tongue literacy is a vital element in the promotion of extended forms of L1/English bilingualism for individual minority language speakers, and consequently for minority language maintenance. And, far from its inclusion in the primary school curriculum detracting from the general education of minority L1 children, it may be expected to enhance such education, by offering earlier access than is now usual to more than one cultural tradition and to alternative conceptual frameworks.

Building on the establishment of mother-tongue literacy, schools could continue to provide minority L1 children with a systematic programme of minority language support as part of the regular school curriculum at primary and secondary levels. Such teaching would, of course, be optional, but whenever possible should take place during normal school hours. The purpose of this instruction would be to consolidate and extend L1 competence, so that pupils' L1/English bilingualism develops in 'additive' rather than 'subtractive' form (see Lambert, op cit). It would include instruction in L1 literacy skills to advanced levels and, where minority language communities use non-standard language varieties, the appropriate related standard languages would be taught. The literature and associated cultural heritage of the minority language would form a substantial component of the teaching. At secondary school and FE levels, such courses would lead to appropriate forms of public examination and certification, developed through the present examination boards and their successors. Any new assessment scheme would have to take into account the special character of this group's minority language competence, giving due weight to oral proficiency as well as literacy skills and cultural knowledge. Both first and foreign language teachers in Britain are currently interested in the development of criterion-referenced procedures for the assessment of communicative competence (oral and written), and towards 'profile' reporting of linguistic attainment. This trend is likely to facilitate the development of assessment schemes for minority languages which validly reflect the proficiency of minority L1 children receiving 'continuation instruction' in schools.

Programmes in minority language teaching of the kind described above are well-established in Britain for the indigenous minority languages, and already exist to some extent for the newer ones. They are also widely provided in other countries. The balance of international experience suggests that such teaching is likely to enhance minority L1 skills, though not normally to the levels attained by literate monolinguals, without in any way hindering the ongoing development of English competence. It is also likely to promote positive attitudes among minority L1 children towards their language and its associated culture.

It is this particular minority language initiative within the mainstream school system which is most directly related to current community-based minority language education. It is therefore vitally important that any development of such teaching in mainstream schools be accompanied by the fullest consultation with the minority language communities, regarding for example, the language varieties to be taught, and the literary and cultural aspects of the programme. The mainstream school system is unlikely to be able to cater for all aspects of the current work of voluntary minority language schools; such schools may therefore be expected to continue to function as a valued element in multi-lingual educational provision. They could benefit from 'official' support of various kinds, as could the mainstream schools from the considerable experience of the voluntary sector.

(3) Minority language learning for monolingual English-speaking children

An important part of any comprehensive education policy for minority languages would be the provision of opportunities for monolingual English-speaking children to learn the language of a local minority language community. Such provision might take different forms, according to local interest, ranging from bilingual pre-school programmes with mixed groups of English Ll and minority Ll children, to the provision of beginners' classes for English Ll children at various stages of primary and secondary education. This could lead to more advanced study of the language(s) and to appropriate schemes of assessment, taking into account the non-Ll character of this group's proficiency. (Models for a variety of such minority L2 programmes and examinations are again to be found in Welsh and Gaelic contexts, with the teaching of Irish in schools in Northern Ireland as an additional example.) At every level, it would be important to exploit opportunities for joint teaching of Ll and L2 learners: the degree to which such groupings are feasible will crucially depend on the kind of training available to teachers of the languages. In case this suggestion should seem quite unrealistic to some modern language teachers, or to teachers of the languages of minority communities, it should be remembered that class teachers in many British primary schools, and secondary teachers of English, for example, have considerable successful experience of working in the same classes with pupils from English Ll and English L2 backgrounds.

The extent and nature of provision of this kind will partly depend on community support, since enrolment in such programmes would have to be on a voluntary basis. An important group interested in such programmes is likely to be children having personal connections with the languages, but who are not themselves minority Ll speakers. However, the trend in mainstream foreign language teaching towards greater flexibility in courses and in certification evidenced by the 'Graded Objectives in Modern Languages' movement (Harding, Page and Rowell, 1981) offers opportunities for minority languages to take their place in a wider mix of short language courses, which could be quite generally available.

Our support for the extension of minority language education to English Ll children rests on our belief that the present multi-cultural character and linguistic heterogeneity of British society requires not only some special provision for minority Ll children, but a wider knowledge in British society generally of the 'new' languages (and of the cultures to which they give access). The exclusive concentration of resources for minority language education on children from the minority communities themselves could result in a degree of ghettoisation - even if such resources were provided within the mainstream education system. On the other hand, the extension of opportunities for minority language learning beyond the communities themselves would increase links between them and the wider society, fostering societal multi-culturalism as well as providing individual English L1 speakers with opportunities to broaden their personal linguistic and cultural horizons in directions relevant to contemporary Britain.

(4) Minority language as medium of instruction

The choice of language for use in school reception, initial literacy, and in 'continuation' minority language teaching, is one aspect of a more general issue: whether the minority language should be used, to any degree, as a medium of instruction for minority L1 children. The fourth minority language educational initiative of potential importance in the British context concerns the extension of minority language use beyond special cases, through the introduction of bilingual minority language/English programmes in primary and/or secondary schooling.

The general experience of children with mother tongues other than English in the mainstream British education system currently approximates to the process described by Swain and others as linguistic 'submersion' (see, for example, Cohen and Swain, 1976). That is, with or without preliminary or concurrent ESL provision, the children have to follow a school programme which assumes native speaker competence in English, and familiarity with English cultural norms. Large numbers of their classmates are likely to be native English speakers, and the pace of work is often geared to native speakers' needs. The teacher is not very likely to speak the minority children's languages, or to be closely familiar with all of their cultural backgrounds.

Such an educational experience has been associated in many research studies with a range of negative outcomes, including low levels of academic achievement and depressed scores on a range of 'intelligence' measures (see review by Swain and Cummins, 1979). It has also been associated with the phenomenon of 'subtractive' bilingualism (see Lambert, op cit). The research evidence on the English proficiency and general academic achievement of minority L1 children in British schools is however somewhat conflicting, with some studies showing lower attainment by minority L1 children, when compared with English L1 children, and others showing no difference (see, for example, Dickinson et al, 1975, and review by Little, 1981). There seems to be no British research evidence regarding the quality of these children's bilingual competence.

Various theoretical arguments are currently being advanced for bilingual programmes for minority groups. For example, reviewing a number of research studies, Swain (1981) concludes that those aspects of linguistic proficiency which are most central to progress and achievement in academic settings are cross-lingual (i.e. are

9

capable of transfer from one language to another). She further claims that education in the first language promotes these language abilities, which are essentially those associated with cognitively demanding tasks in context-reduced situations. Swain therefore, argues that 'early education in the first language provides a solid basis for academic progress in a second language'.

In the British context, the indigenous minority languages apart, there is an almost complete absence of experience against which such arguments might be tested. The prestigious international schools in Europe provide examples of successful bilingual education; the languages principally involved, however, are not among those of Britain's most substantial minority communities.

In some other countries the perceived 'poor academic performance' of minority L1 children taught in majority language medium has been an important factor leading to a degree of official support for some types of bilingual education. In Britain, however, arguments for bilingual education on 'compensatory' grounds have been given very little weight. Extensive provision of this type seems likely to develop in Britain only as part of some wider social movement, committed to promoting multi-culturalism and minority language maintenance. As such its introduction would be symbolic of deep-seated change in British society, and would certainly arouse deep controversy and political debate. On cognitive and linguistic grounds, the arguments for minority language medium education have some weight: perhaps the time has come to face up to the social and political implications.

Principles for minority language education

Having discussed in general terms four types of initiative relating to minority language education in Britain, we set out here some principles which should, in our view, form the basis for the kind of policy on minority languages that we would like to see evolve.

(1) A primary consideration in developing educational policy for minority languages must be the educational needs of children for whom a minority language is the first language of the home.

(2) 'Additive' mother tongue/English bilingualism would be a more satisfactory outcome for minority L1 children, rather than the present common pattern, where English often comes to replace the minority L1 almost entirely.

(3) Consideration must also be given to the range of other languages offered to children for whom English is the home language. Whether or not these children have any immediate

geographical or cultural connection with a minority community, the newer minority languages should be available in addition to the European languages commonly on offer to these children as part of their general education, just as Welsh, Gaelic and Irish are already on offer in appropriate parts of the United Kingdom. This could, of course, most easily be done in the context of the general availability of two languages for all pupils in addition to English.

(4) Minority language communities currently existing within the United Kingdom are entitled to similar consideration with regard to minority language education, without regard to their historical or geographical origins. The allocation of resources for the teaching of minority languages should be through the application of similar criteria across the full range of UK minority languages, although smaller communities, of course, cannot expect to have as great a share of limited resources as do the larger groups.

(5) The development of minority language education policy must be undertaken in the fullest consultation with the minority language communities themselves, and with their involvement at both national and local levels in decision-taking regarding minority language provision.

(6) The promotion of minority language education within the maintained sector must form part of a wider programme for multicultural education. Such a programme would have as a general social goal the legitimation of cultural and linguistic diversity as positive features of contemporary life in Britain.

(7) The requirements of minority L1 children and English L1 children learning the minority language will at times be sufficiently distinctive to necessitate separate instructional provision for groups of differing minority language ability. However, the principle of open access to minority language instruction must be upheld in the schools, with courses at different levels open to all likely to benefit, and not groups.

(8) Any general policy of minority language teaching developed for the UK must take into account the resident, non-migratory character of its contemporary minority language communities. The basis for minority language education proposed in the EC Directive of July 1977, which has been interpreted as seeing the main purpose of minority language teaching as facilitating the reintegration of the children of migrant workers into their country of origin, is of only limited relevance for most minority language communities in the United Kingdom.

ANALYSIS OF NEEDS AND RECOMMENDATIONS FOR ACTION

In the following section we discuss first some of the areas in which progress is being made, but in which further action is needed if progress is to be made towards realising the kinds of principles and policies we have indicated as desirable. We then go on to suggest a mechanism through which further developments might be undertaken.

We shall say very little here about the implications for methods and materials development of initiatives of the first and fourth types outlined earlier. With reference to school reception, the experience of the Bradford Project (MOTET, 1981) is likely to produce very useful guidelines on what is appropriate. As far as the use of minority languages as mediums for later schooling is concerned, Welsh and Gaelic experience would, in terms of similarity of educational context, be the most relevant sources to draw on for large-scale use. In addition, John Wright's World in a city (ILEA Learning Materials Service and Commission for Racial Equality, 1981) materials represent the first fully worked out published bilingual materials in the languages of newer minority communities designed specifically for the British urban context. What follows in this section refers almost exclusively to initiatives of the second and third types mentioned earlier.

It follows from the educational justifications discussed in the previous section for initiatives of our second and third types, and the principle we wish to advance of maximum possible access to the classes, that we envisage at each age-level classes consisting of learners with very varying degrees of experience of the languages concerned, including in certain cases some with none at all. These latter will in some cases be the children and grandchildren of people who used the languages in their everyday lives, but who have not themselves ever learned them. In other cases they will simply be pupils who wish to take the opportunity of learning from scratch a language which has a more immediate reality in the local environment than some of the foreign languages traditionally taught in schools. We are, then, faced with the need to focus on strategies and materials for teaching very heterogeneous classes: it is only rarely that teachers will be able to work on a whole-class basis. They will have instead to plan above all for individual and small- group learning activities, exploiting to the full the possibilities of peer-group learning and guidance from older pupils and of the fact that living contexts for the learning are easily to hand – a resource comparatively neglected even by ESL teachers. The favourable ratio of models to learners which is likely to exist in community language classes should be taken advantage of through the use of interactive, communicative language practice and manipulation; self-study techniques will also need to be encouraged.

It is not appropriate in our Report to set out in full the types of teaching strategy or of materials which are needed; the papers contributed to the Working Party by Arturo Tosi and John Broadbent consider in more detail some of the relevant questions. We confine ourselves here to indicating some of the principles on which methods and materials need to be built and the sources of existing experience and assistance that could usefully be consulted.

In terms of materials, the implications of our definition of the kind of learning groups that are likely include the following:

a) Elementary materials should include more than reading primers appropriate only to learners who have an already well-established command of the oral language. They must include also materials designed for teaching or consolidating the early stages of the spoken language.

b) It would be a mistake to attempt at this stage to recommend exclusively a particular syllabus type. Nevertheless, of the syllabus types available, a topic-centred one has advantages over others, in that it allows for a balance between controlled work with a whole class, group work, and individualisation in order to cater for different learning levels and styles.

c) The initial contextualisation for the language materials needs to be the British urban learning environment, leading on of course to illustration of the language in question in use in the whole range of appropriate environments, including that of the country or countries of origin.

d) The matching of age-level interests and linguistic level needs especially careful attention, since pupils are likely, for example, to be learning to read later than is often assumed by the authors of initial reading primers.

e) The production quality of printed materials should equal that of other learning materials available to the pupil at school, although 'home-made' materials will continue to have their place, as they do in the teaching of all subjects. Illustrations should also be of the highest quality.

f) Again, in the interests of achieving equivalence with the languages more commonly taught in schools, it will be important to develop a full range of audio and visual materials: tapes, both audio and increasingly video, slides, filmstrips, charts, photographs. These are at present hardly available for the languages of most of the minority communities, yet they are the stock-in-trade of modern language and ESL teachers.

g) The changes that take place in any language brought into close contact with another, and used by bilingual speakers, should be more readily accepted by the writers of materials to be used for learning purposes. The positive functions of codeswitching should also be accepted, as part of the ultimate goal of a linguistic repertoire extending from local, anglicised, spoken varieties to standard literary and formal varieties.

What all this implies is a planned programme of development which would draw together the already considerable body of relevant experience. This must come, above all, from existing teachers of the languages of minority communities, who have struggled against the odds for many years, faced the realities of teaching in very difficult circumstances with quite inadequate resources, and produced workable strategies and attractive materials out of very little. However, the experience of ESL teachers in terms of methodologies and materials might also be usefully drawn on. After all, their approaches have often been developed for exactly the same learners, working in the same kind of very heterogeneous groups. English mother tongue teachers have an impressive record in 'humanising' language learning, and relating it to the individual needs and interests of the learners. Perhaps above all in the development of reading and writing skills, and in the relating of linguistic to general cultural learning could secondary English teachers, and indeed general primary teachers with their 'language development' hats on, be extremely useful. Teachers of modern languages have in recent years had to develop new approaches with classes of very mixed motivation and ability; their experience of this, and their wide use of audio-visual materials would be a very valuable resource for teachers of the languages of minority communities. It should be clear that such exchange of experience between different branches of the language teaching profession would certainly not be one-way: teachers of the language of minority communities have a great deal to offer their colleagues, as well as to learn from them.

Teacher training

Facilities for the training of teachers of all but a few of the languages of minority communities in Britain hardly exist at present. Those teachers who have trained to teach the mother tongue in the context of the home country could often benefit from additional preparation for the very different context of British schools, and pupils with varying understandings of the appropriate relationship between teacher and taught. We believe too that there is a need for the kind of recognition of expertise by fellow professionals which comes more easily from the possession of a widely-recognised 'mainstream' qualification.

We recommend therefore that both <u>in-service and initial teacher training courses</u> be developed systematically, for, in the first place, at least the twelve languages which follow, representing probably the most widely-used languages of minority communities:

Bengali, Chinese, Greek, Gujerati, Hindi, Italian, Panjabi, Polish, Portuguese. Spanish, Turkish, Urdu.

As far as <u>in-service training</u> is concerned, we particularly welcome the initiative taken by the Royal Society of Arts in setting up a Working Party on The Training of Teachers of Minority Languages, and that Working Party's recommendation, made on the basis of careful initial soundings about the potential demand for a Certificate in this field, that such a scheme should be developed. Progress with this proposal, leading to the availability of a qualification parallel to the well-established and widely-respected Certificate in the Teaching of English as a Second or Foreign Language, would be the readiest way to promote the development of improved teaching methods throughout the country. We urge the RSA to proceed, and to consider solving some of the undoubtedly difficult problems of viability arising from the wide range of languages involved by means of a close association with some of the existing TESL/TEFL courses and centres, and by accepting the positive benefits of having certain elements in common for teachers of different languages.

In the longer term it will be important to offer <u>initial training</u> too, through PGCE course options in the languages of minority communities in Britain. As with the in-service courses, these would probably fit most easily alongside existing strong departments of modern language teaching, or of English to speakers of other languages. If approaches from appropriate departments to the DES for permission to run such options are not forthcoming, we would like to see the Department take the initiative in locating courses in the different regions.

In both types of course mentioned above, the contact time with students is not likely to exceed 100 hours, with perhaps the same again available in study time and teaching practice. Course content is also likely to be similar, starting from the assumption of a degree or equivalent qualification in the appropriate language, with associated oral and written fluency. (John Broadbent's paper, written for this Working Party, 'Towards a programme of in-service training for teachers of the languages of minority communities in the UK', gives an indication of the kind of range that might be appropriate.) Whatever schemes are evolved, it will be important to see that they give a good deal of emphasis to developing an understanding of the principles underlying language learning and bilingualism, as well as to the design of syllabuses, methods and materials, and to classroom management, all set in an appropriate

context of multi-cultural education for all pupils. To ensure a
continuing flow of entrants to these teacher training courses, it
would also be important to strengthen facilities for A-level and
degree-level study of the languages themselves, the latter in
particular in those departments which are willing to develop an
interest in and contact with the local communities in Britain,
alongside their more traditional specialisms relating to countries
of origin.

Some primary teachers in particular will continue be trained by the
BEd route, and we think that short options similar to those above
should be developed in this context too. These might prepare, for
example, for the use of more than one language in the reception
class for the teaching of literacy in the languages of minority
communities by those students with appropriate existing language
skills; or they might be aimed at both monolingual and bilingual
students with the intention of encouraging positive responses to
linguistic diversity in schools, on the lines being developed by the
Schools Council Mother Tongue Project. In addition, a smaller number
of more substantial, probably BEd, courses will be needed, with an
emphasis on bilingual education of the fourth type discussed earlier
in this Report, drawing perhaps on Welsh and Scottish experience.

Public examinations

Although examinations are likely to affect directly only a minority
of the pupils we would like to see given encouragement to develop
skills in the languages of minority communities, they are nevertheless important in terms of the status that the subjects need to
obtain in secondary and tertiary education, and in the development
of the future teachers of the languages. The Working Party thought
it right therefore to investigate the availability and currency of
such examinations, and a paper by Euan Reid is available separately.
The recommendations from that paper are included here.

a) The Schools Council should reconsider with the individual examinations boards the basic 'supply and demand' policy which most
   of the GCE and CSE boards seem to operate with, and think about a
   longer-term planned approach to provision in this field. Given
   the position in schools and in society generally of many of the
   people involved in teaching these minority languages, it seems
   likely that there is a particular unfamiliarity with the mechanisms for teachers to influence the provision and administration
   of public examinations.

b) Since the limited availability of examinations may lead many
   potential candidates to conclude that there is no 'market value'
   in studying the languages concerned, and to the loss of a
   valuable national resource, those examinations boards already

involved in this field should avoid further reduction in choice, and indeed plan to fill existing gaps and extend the choice of syllabuses available, particularly at A-level. Some mechanism should be found to relieve the boards of the heavy costs of examinations with very small entries.

c) The RSA should be encouraged to follow up its proposals for extending the range of languages at present offered, though these should not be seen as alternatives to GCE/CSE provision for schools.

d) These boards conducting existing examinations, and the regional groupings planning the new 16+ examinations should reconsider the design of such examinations with particular reference to the needs of candidates who are bilingual or potentially bilingual residents of this country and whose families have settled here in the last 50 years. The context of new ideas for modern language examinations in general at 16+ needs also to be borne in mind: otherwise there is a great danger that the study of many of these languages in schools will continue to have a fundamentally different status from the study of French or German. There certainly needs to be greater explicitness in the syllabus, and enough flexibility to allow the possibility of negotiation with particular classes to meet specific needs.

The last three recommendations relate to the 'currency' of exam passes in minority languages for applicants for degree-level courses.

e) Specialist requirements for entry to languages or area studies departments: We suggest that, even where these departments are not teaching the languages concerned, such exam passes should be seen as very positive achievements and as direct evidence of general linguistic and 'inter-cultural' skills.

f) General entrance requirement: We feel that clear guidance needs to be offered to admissions tutors in all departments, with reference to the desirability of giving equal weight to passes in these subjects. They represent at least as clear an academic achievement as the more widely held foreign language passes, particularly given the present heavy emphasis on translation.

g) Distinction between candidates offering such passes as 'mother-tongue' or as 'foreign language': We urge the desirability of an explicit and consistent policy to be operated by all concerned with admissions. The University of London seems to us to offer a useful model in this respect: "A candidate who has been educated in the medium of English can count one of these languages as a foreign language. If, however, his education was not conducted in English, he will be able to count English as a foreign language."

Language development & training units

To provide a focus for the kind of developments we have identified as desirable, we recommend that a number of <u>language development and training units</u> be designated in existing teaching institutions in different parts of the country, again in the first place for the languages we listed earlier.

The function of such units would include:

a) the assembly and evaluation of all existing materials in the relevant language, produced in the United Kingdom or overseas;
b) the development where necessary of further materials and teaching strategies for the full age-range of potential learners, on the basis of the principles outlined in our section on methodologies and materials;
c) the piloting of new and adapted materials in a variety of con-texts, evaluation of their usefulness, and arranging for publica-tion of revised versions;
d) the provision of initial and/or in-service teacher training courses, primary and secondary, including some on linguistic diversity for monolingual teachers;
e) the development of appropriate forms of assessment of language learning, formal and informal;
f) the development of research on language and language learning in bilingual communities in Britain.

In all cases the use of advisory panels, consisting of language-teaching colleagues in neighbouring disciplines, would be important in promoting the maximum cross-fertilisation. In addition, we recommend that an appropriate existing <u>national</u> <u>centre</u> should be given the necessary resources to act as <u>a link</u> between the units working on the various languages, promoting the exchange of experi-ence and ideas between them and the longer-established branches of the language-teaching profession at both primary and secondary level. The United States Government's National Clearinghouse for Bilingual Education provides one model for such an agency.

The obvious location for such units would be in colleges, polytech-nics, universities or LEA centres which had, or were prepared to acquire, expertise in the following:

a) the spoken and written languages, including those varieties used in Britain now;
b) a range of different types of language teaching, and applied linguistics;
c) teacher education and training with a multi-cultural perspective;
d) design and production skills and facilities, or access to them, for printed and other teaching materials.

In some cases it might be necessary to draw on more than one neighbouring institution for the right combination.

To staff these units, existing expertise will provide an excellent basis, but it will probably be necessary to second or offer advanced study opportunities in, for example, bilingual education, applied linguistics, sociolinguistics and language teaching materials design. Some of the existing Masters Degree courses should be encouraged to develop specialisms in these areas.

General LEA and higher education finance is under such pressure at the moment that it is unrealistic to expect that the necessary money will come entirely from 'internal' sources. It will therefore be necessary to look for some pump-priming from, for example:

1. Department of Education and Science
2. The Schools Council
3. Home Office: Section 11
4. Department of the Environment: Urban Aid
5. European Community: Social Fund
6. Private sources, including foundations and publishers

INFORMATION NEEDS FOR LEAs

This section of the Report is based upon the replies of 26 LEAs to our circular letter sent in January 1981 and on subsequent informal discussions with officers of LEAs. The original letter sought to discover the information needs of LEAs faced with the task of responding constructively to the EC Directive 77/486. Some LEAs understood that the Directive applied only to the children of migrant workers from other EC countries; others were aware of the present Government policy to apply the Directive without regard to the country of origin of the children concerned (following the statement of the Secretary of State for Education, 24 March 1980) and yet others felt that the Directive was marginal to their proper concern, namely the application of basic principles of education to the pupil population identified in their schools. The following three lists of needs and concerns derive chiefly from the responses of this last group of LEAs and, in consequence, extend beyond purely informational needs.

Needs to be met by local enquiry

1. Basic information concerning the composition by language and distribution by age and school of the group of pupils concerned. At some stage this basic information will need to be supplemented by information about the oracy and literacy competence of pupils of different ages and in different linguistic groups.

2. Information about the mother tongue skills of bilingual teachers employed by the LEA, together with an indication of their possible interest in undertaking some mother tongue teaching, and of any experience or training they may have had in this area.

3. An estimate of the demand by parents and pupils for mother tongue teaching. This will require a dialogue with ethnic minority groups. It must be noted however that demand often follows availability. Evidence that the LEA acknowledges the value of mother tongue teaching would inevitably stimulate demand. Demand, however, cannot be the major reason for provision. Justification on educational grounds must be paramount. The justification will be different for different age groups and so will be the appropriate response.

4. A knowledge of the extent and diversity of provision of mother tongue teaching by voluntary organisations and by the voluntary, non-timetabled efforts of bilingual teachers in maintained schools. To give effect to the co-operation envisaged in paras. 5 and 11 (below), this information about voluntary effort will need to be specific as to the names of the organisers, location of classes, language taught, and ages and numbers of pupils (see also point 17 below).

5. A knowledge of the ways in which the voluntary organisations feel that the LEA could help them with premises, teaching resources and training courses for their teachers.

Needs to be met from external sources

6. Information about appropriate methodologies for developing mother tongue competence, for teaching through the mother tongue, and for creating in schools a generally supportive context for bilingual pupils uncertain about the value of their first or home language.

7. Information about available teaching materials and materials in process of development. Sources of evaluation of these materials. Knowledge of opportunities for co-operative effort in materials development.

8. Information about in-service training programmes sponsored by other LEAs, teachers' centres and institutions of higher education.

9. Information concerning the availability and suitability of existing public examinations in minority languages and evidence of the current development of better examinations.

10. A synopsis of relevant research findings in the area of mother tongue teaching, especially concerning the impact of mother tongue maintenance on the development of English language skills.

11. Examples of co-operation between LEAs and voluntary organisations in the field of mother tongue teaching with particular reference to ways in which maintained secondary schools, voluntary classes and adult educational institutes might co-operate in the provision of tuition for public examinations. (Our Working Party hopes to make available a number of accounts of such practice.)

12. The most pressing need is for information on administrative and organisational strategies for getting different types of mother tongue learning support efficiently and economically to the points of need, and for most LEAs this means within existing budgets and sources of funding. This need is felt most keenly by those LEAs wishing to apply accepted first and infant school practice of building upon the language skills and experience of pupils entering the school system when many pupils have little or no knowledge of English.

13. A knowledge of the response in other countries to the advent of similarly linguistically diverse populations.

Some tasks to be performed and problems to be solved

14. As with any aspect of the curriculum, the LEA needs to be equipped to judge the quality of what is provided by way of mother tongue or minority language education. This will involve assessing the progress of the pupils, the competence of the teachers both linguistically and pedagogically, the suitability of the teaching material available and used, and the appropriateness of the programme arrangements. The variety of mother tongues to be taught or used as the medium of learning, together with the potentially wide age range of the learners, may pose problems for LEA advisory systems.

15. In a different category, teachers have information needs, some of which LEAs should seek to meet. As one LEA reports, 'teachers need to understand that at present, by default, we allow ethnic minority children to under-value their culture and their language; that in their language they have a great personal, cultural and economic asset which the school much encourage them to prize and develop'.

16. Teachers need more opportunities to acquaint themselves with the elements of some non-European languages. Some adverse comparisons between the teaching methods employed in some voluntary classes and those used in maintained schools are well-founded

but others of these judgements might be seriously modified if a knowledge of certain non-European languages was more widespread amongst teachers.

17. The task of collecting the data referred to in paras. 1, 4 and 5 will be facilitated by the use of the Mother Tongue Teaching Directory developed by the National Council for Mother Tongue Teaching in collaboration with the Linguistic Minorities Project of the University of London Institute of Education; and the Linguistic Minorities Project's Schools Language Survey is intended to provide LEAs with the means to assemble the information referred to in para. 1.

REFERENCES FOR SECTION A

COHEN, A D (1975). A sociolinguistic approach to bilingual education. Rowley, Mass: Newbury House.

COHEN, A D and M SWAIN (1976). Bilingual education: the immersion model in the North American context. TESOL Quarterly 10, p 45–53.

CUMMINS, J (1981). Bilingualism and minority-language children. Toronto, Ontario: OISE.

DEPARTMENT OF EDUCATION AND SCIENCE (1980). Matters for Discussion 11: A view of the curriculum. London: HMSO.

DEPARTMENT OF EDUCATION AND SCIENCE (1981). Directive of the Council of the European Community on the education of the children of migrant workers. London: Department of Education and Science. (Circular 5/81.)

DICKINSON, L, A HOBBS, S M KLEINBERG and P J MARTIN (1975). The immigrant school learner: a study of Pakistani pupils in Glasgow. Slough: NFER.

EKSTRAND, L H (1980). Home language teaching for immigrant pupils in Sweden. International Migration Review. 14, 3 p 409–427.

GARNER, M (ed.) (1981). Community languages: their role in education. Melbourne/Sydney: River Seine Publications.

HARDING, A, B PAGE and S ROWELL (1981). Graded objectives in modern language teaching. London: Centre for Information on Language Teaching and Research.

HORNBY, P A (ed.) (1977). Bilingualism: psychological, social and educational implications. New York: Academic Press.

LAMBERT, W E (1977). The effects of bilingualism on the individual: cognitive and sociocultural consequences. In Hornby, P A (ed.) 1977, p 15–27.

LITTLE, A (1981). Education and race relations in the UK. In: J Megarry, S Nisbet and E Hoyle (eds.) 1981, p 129–143.

LITTLE, A and R WILLEY (1981). Multi-ethnic education: the way forward. London: Schools Council.

MEGARRY, J, S NISBET and E HOYLE (eds.) (1981). World Yearbook of education 1981: education of minorities. London: Kogan Page.

MOTHER TONGUE AND ENGLISH TEACHING PROJECT (1981). Summary of the report — volumes I and II. Bradford: University Education Department.

NATIONAL ASSOCIATION OF LANGUAGE ADVISERS (n.d.). Foreign languages in schools.

ROSIER, P and M FARELLA (1976). Bilingual education at Rock Point: some early results. TESOL Quarterly 10, p 379–388.

SAIFULLAH KHAN, V (1978). Bilingualism and linguistic minorities in Britain: developments, perspectives. Briefing Paper, London: Runnymede Trust.

SWAIN, M (1981). Bilingual education for majority and minority language children. Paper presented at AILA 81, Lund, Sweden.

SWAIN, M and CUMMINS, J (1979). Bilingualism, cognitive functioning and education. Language Teaching & Linguistics: Abstracts vol 12 no. 1, p 4–18.

Section B: Papers by Working Party Members

EDUCATIONAL JUSTIFICATION FOR THE INCLUSION OF
MINORITY GROUP LANGUAGE PROVISION IN STATE SCHOOLS*

Barré Fitzpatrick
Principal Lecturer in Education, Bradford College

We have the tradition in this country, enshrined in and developing
from the 1944 Education Act, of the development of the individual as
the focus of the educational process. Much of the research in education, much of the debate in education and much of the practice in
education has been stimulated by the phrase 'according to his age,
aptitude and abilities'. How this phrase is interpreted depends a
great deal upon the ideological perspective of the interpreter, just
as the implementation of policies appropriate to a particular interpretation depends a great deal upon the constraints operating at any
particular time. However, the individualistic and egalitarian spirit
of the 1944 Act underpins the whole of the education system and
compels us to look beyond a mere description of the curriculum to
the processes involved in a realisation of goals to which we explicitly and implicitly aspire.

In terms of the state school system we can consider goals at three
different levels when we are considering minority groups in schools:

(1) socio-political goals;

(2) educational goals;

(3) linguistic goals.

Evidently these three sets of goals overlap in certain ways but they
nevertheless represent three areas of primary focus for the educa-
tionalist.

(1) Socio-political goals

These are goals which relate to the developing relationships between
different socio-cultural groups in society as a whole and to society's image of itself as a particular kind of multi-racial/multi-
cultural/multi-lingual entity. Various models have been presented
in the literature (1) which indicate the complexity of the area and
the difficulty in producing a comprehensive model which can account
for the wide range of social and political situations and motiva-
tions underlying relationships between groups in a society. These
kinds of goals govern the major decisions relating to educational

provision and language policy in general, since it is at this level that major questions of resource are settled.

(2) Educational goals

Within the socio-political framework there are many educational questions to be resolved which themselves occur at different levels. Perhaps the major question to be addressed is that of equality of educational opportunity and how far existing provision is appropriate to bilinguals from minority groups.   Other questions occur concerning the appropriate provision to be made for both bilinguals and mono-linguals within different units of the system, e.g. the local authority, the school, the classroom; the appropriate structure of the curriculum, assessment and examination, teaching method, staffing and so on. A further set of questions relates to the educational development of the bilingual. How do the different languages work for the bilingual in the educational setting? What is the effect of different sorts of provision? What about the cultural question? Many of these questions, like many other questions in education, cannot be answered definitively but must nevertheless be given a great deal of consideration in establishing goals and priorities for bilingual education programmes.

(3) Linguistic goals

There is a strong relationship between the linguistic goals at the socio-political level and the effect of language provision within school programmes. Linguistic goals within a programme will determine such questions as what languages are used (also what form of language) and for what range of purposes? Are all language skills to be developed in all languages? Decisions have to be made about the range of use of L1 and L2 within the curriculum and within the corporate life of the school. Decisions also have to be made regarding the choices open to each student or pupil. Does a programme offer a one-way or two-way bilingualism, for example? Again there is no easy resolution of goals in this area, and level of resource is a crucial constraint.

An examination of our goals in education may reveal deficiencies in our thinking if we normally operate on the assumption that a certain amorphous, traditional consensus exists by which innovation can be measured.   However, given that our goals may be imprecise and our actions governed in many cases by tradition, there are certain well-founded 'minimal' principles which demand a reappraisal of the place of minority group languages in our schools. The most compelling of these relate to the education of our bilingual children but there are others which concern the education of our monolingual English-speaking children and schools and society at large in ways crucial to our development in a shrinking world.

25

THE EDUCATION OF OUR BILINGUAL CHILDREN

Very many British schools now include in their student population significant numbers of children who have either come to this country having been born abroad, or who are born in this country of parents who speak a language other than English. These children have a command of English which ranges from nil through everyday conversational fluency to native-like ability. Most of these children suffer from a number of labels which have negative associations and carry negative expectations, e.g. 'immigrant' (regardless of place of birth) 'non-English speaker' (regardless of actual ability in English) or 'second language speaker' (often interpreted as 'second-rate language user'). Rarely are such children labelled 'bilingual', a term which is relatively free from negative association. (Perhaps as educators, we ought to think a little more about the labels we use.) In fact, 'bilingual', or in many cases 'multilingual', is a more appropriate description of virtually all children of ethnic minority groups in British schools, and these terms extend our perception of such children in a significant way. One of the consequences of a shift in perception is that we may need to consider what the 'product' of the school system will be. We would accept that schools are geared to producing 'educated' adults. Now, whatever that means in ideological or philosophical terms, in practice it means someone who can read and write their language and who has a sense of cultural identity and continuity. For a bilingual child the educational process should surely be aimed at producing an educated bilingual adult. Yet the present provision in our schools ignores the crucial differences between groups of children in our schools and in particular the powerful and emotive role of language. The language we speak and the variety of language we speak is a powerful marker of the social group with which we identify. It plays a central role in the socialising processes to which we are exposed and at the same time serves to indicate to others what kind of socialisation we are likely to have assimilated. This is the fundamental outcome of the relationship between language: the coding and communication system, and culture: the behaviour and values representative of a particular group (2).

This means that individuals who are identified by appearance or behaviour (including language behaviour) as belonging to a particular group will be expected to behave in accordance with the observer's perceptions of the type of behaviour associated with that group. The observer's perceptions will however tend to accord with the structuring of perceptions (e.g. through attitudes and the mediation of experiences to the child) characteristic of the social group within which he or she has been socialised. The individual's perceptions and attitudes therefore will tend to reflect certain social relationships between different social groups. These relationships, in turn, represent the striving of particular groups for survival: the competition between groups for such things as status, resources, economic or social power. Thus dominant groups will tend to adopt attitudes and patterns of behaviour which overtly or covertly ensure the continuance of that dominance, and non-dominant groups will tend to adopt attitudes and patterns of behaviour to increase their status and command of resources.

The relationships between groups are likely to manifest themselves at an informal level in the attitudes and behaviour of their members, and at a formal level in the organisation and administration of such things as law, education, health, social services, etc. Language plays a significant part in the maintenance of social power: a particular social order, so to speak. This can be seen within English in the way that the specialised language of legal documents or insurance policies maintain the authority of the initiated, or how the less specialised but still convoluted language of the civil service does likewise.

When one considers the use of entirely different languages, the barriers to full participation in the organisation and administration of a society become clearly significant. At an informal level the use of language will indicate in-group/out-group status for the participants, in-group/out-group topics and in-group/out-group attitudes. At the formal, structural level the same is true. Whatever the evidence regarding the specific abilities of bilinguals, it is clear that the socio-political context in which the bilingual has to function exerts strong pressures on how each language is perceived, acquired and used. The status ascribed to a particular language may contribute greatly either to its acquisition or its loss. English is a major world language whose literature is extensive in every field; so much so that the native speakers of English feel no pressure whatever to acquire any other language. This results in a certain insensitivity to the speakers of other languages, particularly minority languages. We tend to feel that the arguments for acquiring the English language are so overwhelming as to be unquestionable. This results in the negative aura which pervades our society with regard to other languages and speakers of other languages. Perhaps we have not been placed in situations where we felt our language threatened often enough. If we had, we might have gained great insight into the strength of the psychological and emotional affiliation we have to our own language. For minority group members there can be enormous pressures to adopt the attitudes of the dominant social group, to identify more closely with it and perhaps to lose a minority language in favour of the socially dominant language. Lambert has referred to this process of language switch as 'subtractive' bilingualism, where bilinguals do not add to their repertoire of linguistic, social and cultural skills by developing productively in both languages ('additive' bilingualism), but are pressured into losing their minority language and the skills and values it represents in favour of adopting, or in many cases attempting to adopt, the language and values of another group.

The individual's response to the status given to his or her language and ethnic culture can be very varied and may change with age and the sorts of experience he has. He/she will tend to move towards one of four positions:

(1) A retreat into national language and culture and a militant stance towards the dominant culture.

(2) A move to adopt the dominant language and culture and reject his or her own.

(3) A state of confusion, a feeling of not belonging to either group.

(4) Bilingualism with biculturalism.

How far the majority of minority group members manage to reach a state of bilingualism with biculturalism, at what age and through what experiences, warrants serious investigation (see Paulston 1975, 1978; Mercer and Mercer, 1979) but for a society to become healthily bilingual, appropriate status needs to be given in social and structural terms to the mother tongues of its members. Moreover, if a society is serious in its response to the bilingualism of many of its members, it should consider social and structural support for 'two-way' bilingualism, i.e. minority   majority group, rather than 'one-way' bilingualism minority group   majority group.

Our first consideration therefore should be the qualities necessary for an 'educated' bilingual. The two dimensions are not necessarily the same since it is possible, as we do largely at present, to promote 'élitist' bilingualism while at the same time denying the living languages of groups within our society.

Our next consideration should be the process of education itself and factors which we believe significantly affect that process. There are three cardinal issues here which relate to the education of minority group children:

(1) home/school links

(2) learning process

(3) language development

(1) <u>Home/school links</u>

Since Douglas', (1964), classic study followed up by Plowden, (1967), the crucial importance of home background and the relationships between home and school has been stressed. This has in the last fifteen years led to development in play-school and nursery provision (subsequently cut back of course), a variety of home-school links in first schools including parental involvement in school activities, and the development of extensive pastoral systems in secondary schools. It is sad that, in 1981, many schools and certainly most parents see home-school relationships as a one-sided affair which means parental support for and compliance with the authority of the school. The work of Midwinter in Liverpool and the community-related Head Start programmes in the USA underlined the benefits of genuine community involvement. How, in the environment provided by the school, does the school indicate a genuine regard for the affiliations and characteristics of the community it serves and the whole society it serves?

This same point relates very strongly to the intention of most schools to maximise the learning potential of each of their pupils as far as possible. The school is a key agent in the development of the growing child's self-image and many research studies have indicated the crucial significance of the self-concept as a factor in the learning process. Yet for minority group children to succeed in school they must either reject the values of their family and community and adopt their teachers' as his prime source of self esteem or they must keep a clear division between those instrumental aspects of the school situation which both home and school applaud (examination success) and those value aspects of school which indicate the worthlessness of their family and community background (racism in books, 'languages' means white languages, etc.). The importance attributed to a child's language and culture in a school may have a considerable effect on his or her school performance.

(2) Learning process

In terms of the learning process it is interesting to see indications in the literature on bilingualism of factors emerging such as cognitive flexibility (e.g. Lambert, 1972 and after) and the instrumental relationship between L1 and L2 (e.g. Rees and Fitzpatrick, 1981). The ability to use alternative perceptions derived from other languages and cultures has a genuine instrumental value for many bilingual children and at the same time is traditionally accepted as a cultural ideal underlying modern language teaching (e.g. Schools Council W.P. 19). In denying a bilingual approach in our schools we are not only helping to suppress a positive facility in our bilingual children, we are denying our monolingual children the opportunity provided by the interaction of alternative perceptions.

(3) Language development

There has been a considerable body of literature developed concerning the language development of children and the ways in which the educational process both inside and outside schools helps, hinders and depends upon the development of language skills in the individual. It is widely accepted that language plays a crucial role in formal education both in terms of the development of the child's intellect and in terms of the social processes involved in schooling and assessment. As a result there has emerged a conviction, universally accepted in first schools and widely acclaimed in secondary schools, that teachers must

(a) accord value to and take proper account of the language skills which the child brings to school

(b) actively seek to develop those skills to enable the child to function linguistically as an educated adult.

What then of the case of the minority group child? Certainly a major characteristic of these children in our schools is that for most of them, English is, in some sense, a second language. Since schooling, and all other major forms of social exchange in this country are likely to continue to be mediated in English to a very large extent, it is imperative that all children learn the means of communication which is a pre-requisite for access to opportunity in our society. Therefore we, as educators, need to take particular account of areas of possible difficulty which speakers of other languages may encounter either in learning the language system or in coping with its demands when it is used in school. In many instances, of course, native speakers of English will have difficulty with the same sorts of areas; sometimes for the same sorts of reasons. However, while we have become accustomed in recent years to have close regard to the resources which children bring to school learning, we have tended to ignore crucial aspects of bilingual children's abilities, in particular their other language and the values and perceptions it encodes for them. Often, as teachers, we are unaware of our pupils' other languages. We may not even know what other language or languages they speak and write. What is more significant in some cases is the fact that we assess our children in school through their use of English; the questions they ask, the comments they make, the answers they give.

Bilingual children in this country may have whole areas of experience coded in terms of spontaneous concepts in a language other than English. They may also have some spontaneous concepts coded in English. At school, however, where most of their 'scientific' concepts are acquired, they must use English. In a sense, if they are successful language learners, they have an advantage here. Since the acquisition of scientific school concepts is largely a symbolic activity, for bilingual children it can become a language-learning activity. In this way, provided they are sufficiently competent in English to cope with the language learning load, they can acquire sets of concepts by instruction and where the system of assessment closely follows the pattern of instruction they can behave successfully. The danger is, however, that their learning remains 'situation specific'. In order to acquire concepts in a real sense, the children must be able to integrate school concepts with their spontaneous concepts at the appropriate level of development. For bilingual children this means not simply interaction between concepts but also interaction between languages. In other words, they have a problem of translatability. While in theory translatability is not a serious problem, in that most people would accept that meanings can be translated from one language to another, in practice bilingual children may not be able to go beyond a simple referential translation and may in fact prefer not to translate at all.

The lack of integration in the conceptual system of a bilingual child may result in what Finnish researchers term 'semilingualism' or the inability to use either language adequately (Skutnaab-Kangas, 1978, 1980). Many researchers believe that a threshold level of competence is necessary in the first language for successful acquisition of a second (e.g. Cummins, 1976). Certainly, recent work (Rees and Fitzpatrick, 1981) underlines the developmental relationship between the first and second languages at the same time as demonstrating that time spent on the first language does not detract from effective acquisition of the second, i.e. English. (A similar point was made for foreign languages in Schools Council W.P. 19.)

There are many detailed and complex questions to be considered here, but the weight of the linguistic argument lies firmly behind the recognition and provision of minority group languages in the state system.

In concluding this short paper it is perhaps appropriate to consider the benefits of the adoption of minority group languages by the state system in a broader context. Increasingly, with the development of the Third World, multilingual competence will become commonplace. It is doubtful if the present major world languages will be displaced, but it is certainly likely that other languages will emerge to serve in specific world theatres. It is imperative that Britain recognises in real terms that it is a multi-racial and multi-lingual society in order to participate fully in world affairs. It is also imperative therefore that the ideals of modern language provision in schools, both cultural and instrumental, be extended to include a major resource both for the process and in the outcome, i.e. minority group languages. Much of the difficulty in the teaching of modern languages in relative isolation from their cultural context can be overcome if the ethos of the school is multilingual. The basis for the acquisition of competence in any 'other' language is thereby strengthened immeasurably.

NOTES

1. See for example:

   Fishman, J A, ed: <u>Bilingual education: current perspectives.</u> Centre for Applied Linguistics, 1977.

   Spolsky, B: <u>The language education of minority children.</u> Newbury House, 1972.

   Paulston, C B: Education in a bi—multilingual setting. <u>Inter-national Review of Education,</u> vol XXlV no. 3, 1978, p 309–28.

   Tosi, A: Mother tongue teaching for the children of migrants. <u>Language Teaching & Linguistics: Abstracts,</u> vol 12 no. 4, 1979. p 213–231.

2. Levi–Strauss (1963) defined 'Culture' as a 'fragment of humanity which, from the point of view of the research at hand...presents significant discontinuities in relation to the rest of human-ity'. This relates closely to the definition which Schermerhorn (1970) takes from Gordon:

   'Culture signifies the ways of action learned through social-isation, based on norms and values that serve as guides or standards of that behaviour'.

   It is this orientation–behaviour characteristic of the norms and values of an identifiable group which informs our use of the word 'culture'.

REFERENCES

CUMMINS, J (1976). <u>The influence of bilingualism on cognitive growth.</u> University of Alberta.

DOUGLAS, J W B (1964). <u>The home and the school.</u> MacGibbon and Kee.

LAMBERT, W E and G R Tucker (1972). <u>The bilingual education of children.</u> Newbury House.

LEVI–STRAUSS, C (1963). <u>Structural anthropology.</u> New York: Basic Books.

MERCER, N and L Mercer (1979). Variation in attitudes to mother-tongue and culture. <u>Educational Studies Journal,</u> vol 5 no. 2, June 1979.

PAULSTON, C B (1975). <u>Ethnic relations and bilingual education: accounting for contradictory data.</u> (Working Papers in Bilingualism, 6). Ontario Institute for Studies in Education. p1-44.

PAULSTON, C B (1978). Education in a bi/multilingual setting. <u>International Review of Education</u>, vol XXIV.

PLOWDEN, B et al (1967). <u>Children and their primary schools.</u> HMSO.

REES, O A and F Fitzpatrick (1981). Reports of the mother tongue and English teaching project. Vols I and II, Bradford University. Unpublished.

SCHERMERHORN, R A (1970). <u>Comparative ethnic relations.</u> New York: Random House.

SCHOOLS COUNCIL (1979). <u>Development of modern language teaching in secondary schools.</u> HMSO. (Working Paper 19.)

SKUTNAAB-KANGAS, T (1978). Semilingualism and the education of migrant children as a means of reproducing the caste of assembly line workers. In: Dittmar, Netal.

DITTMAR, Netal (1978). <u>Papers from the first Scandinavian-German Symposium on the language of immmigrant workers and their children.</u> Roskilde Universitets Center.

SKUTNAAB-KANGAS, T and P Toukomaa (1978). <u>Semilingualism and middle class bias.</u> (Working Papers in Bilingualism 19.) Ontario Institute for Studies in Education. p 182-197.

* This paper is a revised version of a contribution prepared originally in 1981 for the Working Party on <u>The Languages of Minority Communities.</u>

TOWARDS A RATIONALE *

Otto Polling
Thomas Gray Centre, (Berkshire LEA), Slough

'Member states shall, in accordance with their national circumstances and legal systems, and in co-operation with the States of
origin, take appropriate measures to promote, in co-ordination with
normal education, teaching of the mother tongue and culture of the
country of origin for the children referred to in Article 1 - EC
Directive on the education of children of migrant workers, 1977.

This Working Party was set up as a result of the acceptance that
there is a range of languages in use among ethnic and cultural
minorities in Britain that as yet are not recognised in our society
generally and in education in particular as a resource to be cher-
ished and nurtured for the benefit of individuals and of the wider
community.

The importance of their languages to the continuing coherence and
developing contribution of ethnic communities in the life of the
nation as a whole is increasingly recognised by the communities
themselves, but only very gradually realised and grudgingly conceded
by the wider society.

Language diversity - aspects of the recent debate.

That Britain is a multi-lingual society with a wide diversity of
languages and dialects spoken and used by people of all ages in
diverse minority communities throughout the country is an incontro-
vertible fact. It has been so for a very long time, of course, but
for historical, political and social reasons the nation has ignored
this fact and viewed itself as a homogeneous, monolingual entity.

Recent history has changed the political, social and economic circumstances of the nation both at home and internationally, and the
cultural and linguistic diversity of the communities that contribute
to the life of the nation has become an issue of concern that can no
longer be swept aside with impunity.

The Bullock Report, A language for life, in 1975 recognised in its
concern for the linguistic development of children at school that,
for 'immigrant children' it is 'a long process...that consists
primarily of learning to live in or between two cultures, and of
learning to handle two languages or dialects' (20.2) and goes on to
recognise further that 'no child should be expected to cast off the
language and culture of the home as he crosses the school threshold,

nor to live and act as though school and home represent two totally separate and different cultures which have to be kept firmly apart" (20.5). Since then the issue of bilingualism and language diversity in the schools and communities of Britain has been increasingly a topic of educational debate.

The conference on Bilingualism in British Education called by CILT in 1976 expressed the view that 'Parity of esteem for languages and culture should be encouraged'. (CILT report: Bilingualism and British education - the dimensions of diversity, 1976; Conclusions, Group B.) It also revealed the paucity of information about the languages and minority groups in Britain and the lack of research in Britain into the educational aspects of bilingualism. The adoption of the EC Directive in 1977 temporarily introduced economic and political considerations into the discussions that clouded the central issue of educational provision in the context of linguistic diversity. At the same time it gave further impetus to the development of action programmes and research projects, viz. the Linguistic Minorities Project, University of London (sponsored by the DES to survey the patterns of bilingualism among minority communities in selected areas of England), the Mother Tongue and English Teaching Project, University of Bradford & Bradford College (funded by the DES to assess a bilingual education programme with primary reception children), and recently the Schools Council Mother Tongue Project.

However, the debate has yet to reach a wider public, both among professional teachers and linguists and among education policy makers and the general public.

A cautious awareness is expressed in the (1980) HMI Series, Matters for Discussion 11, A view of the curriculum:

'There is also a strong case for a modern language in the education of pupils, and for the establishment of national policy on the place of individual languages in the system. Account has also to be taken of the presence in many schools of British born pupils from ethnic minority groups who are already acquainted with languages other than English...who wish to maintain and develop their mother tongues' (Proposition 9).

In view of this caution and careful circumspection of the issue it was refreshing to note the Secretary of State's declaration in his opening speech at the EC Colloquim in March 1980:

'First let me stress that we intend to apply this Directive without regard to the country of origin of the children concerned. That means that we will be concerned about provision for about 650,000 pupils, only a small proportion of whom will be from community countries'.

Since then the Directive has come into force (July 1981) and not only have schools, authorities and the government shown scant movement towards its realisation, but Parliament in its Fifth Report from the Home Affairs Committee (1981) explicitly remarks:

> 'We are not convinced either that a local education authority is under any obligation to provide mother tongue teaching or that it is necessarily in the general interest that they should do so' (Recommendation 40 - ref. para 151).

In the wider society clearly the attitude that 'does not recognise or accord value to the culture and language of children of minorities' still prevails (V Khan, Bilingualism and minority languages in Britain, 1978).

It is against this backcloth of societal factors that this paper endeavours to delineate some of the basic issues at stake in the concern for the maintenance of the languages of minority communities in Britain, and the educational implications involved.

The language issue in a multilingual society

Culturally Britain has perhaps never been a wholly homogeneous nation. Constitutionally it embraces four historic peoples and these themselves trace their origins to various roots and have severally absorbed arrivals from abroad. It is significant that while these peoples have been unified in the use of the English language, their own language traditions have not entirely disappeared and indeed in a number of cases continue to flourish or experience a revival. Some distinctive elements of cultural identity are evidently preserved that have ensured the survival of the distinctive communicative patterns of these languages. In the case of more recent arrivals into British society, it is to be expected that distinct ethnic groups with distinctive cultures will feel a need to maintain their values and traditions, and the medium in which these are most appropriately and effectively expressed, their community language.

To the people of these communities their language or dialect represents an essential part of their personality and cultural identity, the medium in which they express their deepest thoughts and feelings and through which they maintain their cultural and ethnic traditions. Within the minority community the language of the family and home is essential for effective communication between the generations, thus ensuring the maintenance of a mutual understanding and awareness of shared cultural values.

Beyond these bounds the use of the community language as a medium of interpretation of the wider society preserves and develops that language within the community as a living resource able to respond to the wider needs of communication, understanding and expression of the whole community in all spheres of life. The continuing use of the language of the community moreover preserves communication with the country of origin and the whole network of communities across the world who speak that language.

Such links are of more than parochial importance in as much as they present avenues of closer international political, cultural and commercial co-operation. To the wider society knowledge of these languages represents an avenue of access to sharing in an understanding of the rich cultural heritage of these diverse communities and of fuller participation in the developing economies so closely related to this nation's future.

These links and avenues are under threat in a society that views its national language as the only valid vehicle for thought and communication within the nation and with the wider world and continues to perceive assimilation into "the British way of life" as the only pattern of association of other communities acceptable to that society.

Within such a narrow perception of world relations those links are likely to remain only neo-colonial avenues of exploitation. For true benefit and growth the nation must develop an acceptance of its pluralist, multicultural nature and the democratic principle of equality and brotherhood within a free society.

Language maintenance and development needs

To ensure the preservation and development of these rich linguistic resources within our present society it will be necessary to consider how the continued use and exploration of these languages within the context of a pluralist, multicultural and multilingual society may best be promoted.

Basic to this must be the development of language awareness in the nation as a whole, an awareness of the role of language in the personal, social, economic and cultural life of individuals and communities for their identity and survival. An awareness of the different ways language embodies the values and relationships of human society in different contexts and cultures carries the potential of creating an understanding acceptance of the richness inherent in a multicultural society. This implies a need not only for the promotion of bilingualism and multilingualism for minority communities but the development of a comprehensive language awareness policy throughout the nation - a dual programme for the entire education system, both statutory and voluntary.

In respect of this basic requirement for the development of a healthy climate for the appreciation of linguistic diversity the NCLE and its constituent bodies will need to promote the development of language study programmes on as wide a scale as possible, certainly within all teacher training and professional courses and at secondary education level. This task will need to be explored and developed in other committees of the NCLE and relevant constituents.

Within the remit of this working party the task is specifically directed at the implications of the present situation of the languages in use among minority communities for schools and LEAs, and to consider what action is necessary for their more effective development and exploitation for the benefit of pupils and the wider community.

There is no full national survey of the present situation with regard to the languages of minority communities, either in respect of a listing of those languages, the size and distribution of the communities using them or the relative proficiency of school age members of these communities.

Comment from these communities voices anxiety over a decline in the competence of young persons in the languages of their ethnic communities and there is concern for the breakdown of (minority language) communication in the ethnic groups and for the continuity of the use of minority languages in the communities.

Lack of opportunity to develop the full use of the language of the community in the full context of their daily lives is compounded by the increasing dominance of English as the essential vehicle for communication in the wider society and in the learning processes of the classroom.

To maintain the life of those languages in the minority communities the children of these communities will need to develop the use of those languages in parallel with their general cognitive development and alongside their acquisition of English as a second language.

> 'Children must of necessity maintain a continuing balance between their acquisition of English and their ability to communicate freely in their mother tongue. They can't just choose one and neglect the other. Both are essential parts of their social existence and need careful attention if they are to achieve their educational potential.'

> 'The linguistic dimension of family life should be seen as an essential link between home and school. The functioning of two languages in this unrelated pattern - one at school, one at home and never the twain shall meet - cannot be justified on any rational grounds'. (Ram Kaushal - Mother tongue as an issue of importance, CRE Education Journal, 3.2.1981.)

To build on the abilities of pupils in our schools at present some supplementary programmes of mother-tongue teaching will need to be undertaken. This requires that schools and LEA's recognise the existence and validity of the languages of minority communities represented within their areas, accepting that they are a legitimate and essential part of a person's individual and cultural identity. Such recognition will be a first step towards rectifying the personal and social abuse that at present neglects this reality and results in the breakdown of community cohesion and personal relations and the relative educational under-achievement of a large section of the child population.

> 'In order to recognise the value of these languages as essential to an individual's cognitive and social growth, measures must be taken without further delay to provide for their use, develop-ment and teaching in all appropriate forms throughout the state education system'. (NAME Policy Statement: <u>Mother tongue and minority community languages in education</u>, 1981).

Such recognition further requires the schools and LEAs to make them-selves aware of the linguistic diversity and relative distribution of the population they serve, on the one hand, and to explore the degree of linguistic competence of the pupils from the minority communities in their respective languages on the other hand. A survey of the former kind can be developed along lines explored by the Linguistic Minorities Project.

To assess what specific needs exist within the various categories of pupils for the several languages involved it will be necessary to plot the proficiency profile of the pupils within a matrix of complementary factors. These factors will include on the one hand the skills aspect of linguistic proficiency (listening and reading comprehension, oral and writing competence) and, on the other, the level of conceptual sophistication achieved within the language, while also taking into account the spheres of operation accessible to the individual within this profile.

In order to understand the learning opportunities accessible to the various categories of pupils, it will also be useful to survey the existing provision at home and on a voluntary, statutory or incid-ental basis, for the learning of these languages, again taking into account the spheres of operation made accessible by such provision. For voluntary schemes NCMTT is collecting comprehensive details for its Mother Tongue Teaching Directory.

This kind of profiling will make it possible to explore the complex linguistic sophistication and growth of individuals in respect of their mother tongue as well as their second language and thus assess the nature and extent of their bilingualism. Bilingual development of children of minority community backgrounds is by no means uniform or consistent and shows widely variant patterns. While some grow up in a bilingual home setting, where both the minority language and English are used, many grow up initially as monolingual speakers of the minority language/community dialect only, to enter schools where only English is spoken and they are rendered speechless and made aliens to their own locality.

Here the children are expected to acquire the language of the majority society as nationals of this country, while some will be expected by their family also to acquire further competence, i.e. to learn to speak, read or write, in their community's regional or national language.

At present, provision for a balanced development of bilingual oracy and literacy for members of minority communities is virtually nonexistent in Britain. Voluntary schemes initiated and supported by minority community organisations provide limited facilities in some minority languages. Incidental provision by private language schools offers opportunities of a kind, while embassy-run classes make available a range of provision for their nationals. None of these schemes are as yet conceived as participating in an organically integrated policy of educating the bilingual individual. Just so, no statutory provision as yet recognises the need to develop a bilingual dimension to the education in schools of children of ethnic minority origins.

The development of a policy for bi/multilingualism in a multi-ethnic society requires the conscious acceptance within that society of the languages of minority communities as an integral part of the personal development and fulfilment of all members of such communities at all stages and ages of their development.

The education perspective

In a society such as exists in Britain there is a basic framework for educational development and fulfilment of its people outlined in the Education Act of 1944. Section 7 of this Act designates the statutory system of public education to comprise the three progressive stages of primary, secondary and further education and declares the duty of the local education authority to be 'to contribute towards the spiritual, moral, mental and physical development of the community by securing that efficient education throughout these stages shall be available to meet the needs of the population of their area'. Section 8 further elaborates this duty in respect of primary and secondary provision to require 'for all pupils opportunities for education offering such variety of instruction and training as may be desirable in view of their different ages, abilities and aptitudes...including practical instruction and training appropriate to their respective needs'.

As indicated earlier the 'abilities and aptitudes' of ethnic minority pupils and 'their respective needs' in relation to languages of minority communities are as yet rarely taken into account by the statutory education services of local authorities.

In considering the educational implications of a policy for the maintenance and development of bilingualism for ethnic minority pupils in the statutory system, it will be necessary to distinguish appropriately their abilities, aptitudes and needs according to their different ages. It will also be necessary to recognise the context of the educational philosophy within which this policy is developed.

At the same time it will be necessary to consider that this policy development is one major element in the review of educational provision in respect of the needs and requirements of a pluralist, multicultural Britain.

Perhaps it is appropriate at this point to recall some of the basic tenets of educational philosophy upon which our education system rests. It would seem fair to claim that schools aim to produce educated adults, equipped with the knowledge, skills and attitudes that will enable them to develop their aptitudes and capacities to the benefit of society and their personal fulfilment as responsible citizens.

It is the view of what constitutes 'the benefit of society' and 'personal fulfilment' that determines what knowledge, skills and attitudes are seen as relevant to the aims of those who provide the education programme.

In a pluralist, multicultural society the values which shape the view of what constitutes the benefit of society and personal fulfilment are drawn from a wider range of cultural and sub-cultural traditions than has been the case in a mono-cultural society. A consensus of what values are commonly shared needs to be agreed, upon which to reformulate the definitions of benefit and fulfilment in such a way that educational aims and the judgement of relevant knowledge, skills and attitudes are clarified.

Central to the development of the education programme in this view of education stands the individual child, a person with individual aptitudes, capacities and needs. It is this person's cognitive and affective development that concerns those who teach the child.

In a society which comprises communities with diverse languages/cultures children will initially develop their understanding of and response to their environment in terms of the language/culture of their home and community. It is this capacity for understanding and response they bring to school and it is this specific linguistic/

cultural resource upon which the educational development of the children needs to be based.

In the case of a child from the majority population development will initially move towards a monolingual goal, but (one may hope) with an awareness of the linguistic and cultural plurality of the wider world, that will lead to an acceptance of the validity of additional competence in other languages as avenues of access to that plurality.

In the case of a child from a minority community development will eventually move towards a bilingual goal, as both the community and wider society define the educational aims for this child. In the process of developing the aptitudes of this child, his/her initial linguistic resources should form the basis for both cognitive and affective growth. It is perhaps a matter of judgement at which point or stage of development it is appropriate or expedient to begin to graft upon this stock a linked programme of bilingual education. It is, however, essential to the balanced education of a bilingual child to cater for both the first and second language equally in respect of conceptual and creative development.

Ideally the education of the child is a co-operative process shared between the home and the school. Traditionally the school has represented the role of the larger community in this shared process. In the more complex society of today the process of education is necessarily shared by a third partner: the cultural community of the child's parentage. This both complicates and simplifies the sharing of the educational task. For while the legitimate desires of minority communities for an education in accord with the needs and aspirations of their children must shape the educational programme provided, the communities themselves offer a rich resource for the fulfilment of those needs and the wider requirements of an adequate programme of education for a multicultural society. It is a matter of discretion and development how the co-operation and interplay of home, community and school resources may be fostered. Essential to this process is the establishing of effective links between these three partners in the educational enterprise.

Patterns of provision in schools

In respect of the position of the languages of minority communities in the education of the children concerned, adequately bilingual members of the minority communities can play an important role in ensuring the success of the co-operative venture. At primary school level bilingual adults, be they parents, older brothers or sisters, relatives or friends, can greatly help to facilitate a bi/multi-lingual environment for learning. In the nursery and infant school they can contribute as classroom assistants who speak and understand the language and the culture from which ethnic minority children operate. They can play a part in such activities as story telling, both from their community store and in making accessible the wider range of traditions to all children. They can talk to children and engage with them in their activities, contributing both to the maintenance and development of the mother tongues as well as to concept formation and the building of a bilingual vocabulary and language development.

At the same time this shared input can create a multilingual environment within which all children can experience the validity of a variety of languages operating equally for different people and groups.

At later stages it will be appropriate to introduce the skills of reading and writing. Again it must be a matter of judgement which script or type of writing is introduced first, or whether scripts be presented in parallel. The communities could be drawn into this development for the provision both of appropriately staged reading materials and practical tuition in the art of writing. And the materials for reading need not be narrowly restricted to recreational matter. John Wright's workcards produced for the ILEA Bilingual Education Project The World in a City show that materials can equally well be developed to provide bilingual learning resources in support of other areas of curriculum, thus ensuring a balanced bilingual advance that makes the wider learning environment accessible to formulation in both languages. At the secondary level such access to bilingual teaching materials should continue to enhance the bilingual development of the pupils concerned. Here, furthermore, the languages of minority communities should be accorded parity of esteem and provision within the humanities or language department.

For the bilingual child at this stage both the language of its community and English are equally important as life skills, giving access to the cultures and socio-economic life of both communities. Full development of this access should therefore be secured in time-tabled provision and examination options without detriment to opportunities in regard of other subjects, including other (modern) languages. At secondary level, moreover, the availability of instruction in languages of minority communities opens opportunities also for other than minority pupils to have experience of these languages as valid modern language alternatives.

If the purpose of teaching modern languages is to teach young people how to learn another language and gain accesss to another people's culture and way of life, it would make sense in multi-cultural Britain to consider the case for one or other of the modern languages that serve the life and culture of some of our local communities that are so readily accessible for direct, live contact. Such a consideration could be a first and most fertile step towards a greater diversification of modern language teaching in our schools. It would also link naturally with the move towards the introduction of language study as a basic element in the humanities area.

It must be clear that in the development of the partnership between home, communities and school the treatment of how the languages of the minority communities are taught and developed alongside English will need to be formalised and guided in close contact with the development of the whole education programme offered in schools. Only by such formalisation can a situation be reached where there is a framework for the development in these languages of standardised forms in terms of the situation of these communities and their social context within the wider society.

Further provision

Beyond school, in further, adult and in higher education provision also will need to be made in respect of these languages. At colleges of further education and adult education institutes courses in the languages of local minority communities should offer opportunities for adults to acquire a lost ability in the language of their community, or to develop literacy in it. For the general public, courses in these languages might be offered as a useful second/ foreign language skill in support of work or for the pleasure of communication and access to the cultures within our society.

At the level of higher education colleges and university departments shall have to develop a network of provision for advanced study of the languages of minority communities to degree level in support of the general provision for bilingualism. Similarly, these institutions and other bodies in the field shall need to develop provision for the study of these languages to acquire appropriate teaching qualifications, either within the scope of initial training, or in postgraduate or in-service courses.

It is towards such comprehensive provision throughout the education system that we must look in developing the overall rationale and detailed outlines for the teaching and maintenance of the languages of minority communities.

*   This paper is a revised version of a contribution prepared originally in 1981 for the Working Party on The Languages of Minority Communities.

MATERIALS FOR MOTHER-TONGUE TEACHING IN THE CONTEXT OF SECOND LANGUAGE LEARNING - CRITERIA FOR DESIGN AND EVALUATION *

Arturo Tosi
Oxford Polytechnic

INTRODUCTION

In the recent growth of interest and discussions on 'mother-tongue teaching' and 'minority languages in education', a major part of this debate, especially among teachers, has involved the question of appropriate teaching material. While various and conflicting arguments have developed in support of different methodologies, approaches and criteria, it is clear that they are normally derived from the two major areas of language in education: mother-tongue development and second/foreign language acquisition. This paper neither intends to challenge the arguments pertaining to these two areas of learning, nor to add new practical guidelines to the already rich literature on the preparation of syllabuses and materials for language pedagogy in general. Instead, it aims to take a closer look at some particular learning conditions inherent in the process of developing competence in a minority language: something which we attempt to analyse as a process of 'mother-tongue development in the context of second language learning'. Following the definition of this perspective, this study will present a model, or theoretical framework, to analyse some important variables relevant to the planning of the course (what language, curriculum, objectives) and to the structuring of the materials (age group, initial competence, skills/subjects). Finally, a brief discussion will outline some questions relating to the cultural content of the material, its relationship with the linguistic component and its possible implications for the maintenance of the minority culture.

MOTHER TONGUE DEVELOPMENT IN THE CONTEXT OF SECOND LANGUAGE LEARNING

Perspective

The debate questioning the principles of monolingual schooling for linguistically diverse children and its cultural and social implications for a school and a community which claim to have abandoned forced assimilation policies, has produced one of the most important movements in the education of ethnically mixed societies. Since the mid '60s discussions, research and reforms on this subject have developed at an increasing rate in the US and Canada, where they have adopted the term 'bilingual education'. The alternative provision suggested consisted of a system offering simultaneous teaching in both ESL and the children's Ll: the two languages being referred to as those of the 'majority' and the 'minority' groups. In the US the minority group, depending on the particular community served by the school, could refer respectively to indigenous Indian populations, non-Anglo Saxon immigrants, or Hispano migrants from neighbouring countries. In Canada it refers to both indigenous minority populations in either French or English schools, and the children of immigrants attending the mainstream – either English or French – medium schools. The debate in these two countries has led to the US Bilingual Education Act of 1968 for the non-English speaking population, and to the Federal policy of multiculturalism in Canada.

More recently, a similar debate has developed in northern European countries where large numbers of foreign workers are employed. Here, under the increasingly popular title 'mother-tongue teaching' research projects and pilot schemes concerned with the first language of immigrants' children have emerged. In Europe, although initial interest was stimulated by UNESCO and the Council of Europe, a major impetus to the debate was provided by the 1977 EC Directive on the education of children of migrant workers.

In the development of these discussions it soon became apparent that unlike the studies concerned with the teaching of traditional foreign languages in the curriculum, investigations in this area were faced with a complex of societal questions and educational problems of a highly interdisciplinary nature. Significantly, discussions and research on bilingualism and bilingual education, or 'mother-tongue teaching', have concentrated on two separate but interdependent levels. Some scholars have tended to focus on the new status of minority languages and their culture-carrying nature in a society looking for alternatives to the melting-pot hypothesis. Others have concentrated on the therapeutic effect of teaching in the first language, on the linguistic- cognitive development of children who are poor/non-speakers of the majority/school language.

For both goals the particular task of the applied linguist is to offer suggestions towards the development of effective individual bilingualism by providing competence in the mother tongue in the particular context of second language learning. In particular, recent American appraisals of the implications of the 1968 Bilingual Education Act – as well as studies by scholars from the more bilingually equipped Canadian states and the more monolingual-oriented European countries – have demonstrated the necessity and interdependence of the two short-term aims of

(a) individual bilingual competence

(b) community language confidence

to construct a long-term policy of societal multilingualism.

The first provides the basis for the community members to achieve relaxed bilingual conditions leading to situations of stable diglossia, while the second, which results from stabilised diglossia in the environment, is necessary to provide the favourable conditions of exposure, stimulation and motivation for the minority community members to seek and maintain individual bilingualism.

Increasingly, the attention of studies concerned with societal bilingualism and education have focused on the mechanism necessary to achieve these two interdependent conditions, without which, scholars consistently agree, there can be neither serious nor honest talk of equal opportunities in a school and society claiming to pursue multiculturalism as an alternative to assimilation. It is significant that most scholars who discuss bilingual education from different disciplinary viewpoints have incorporated in their perspectives a strong concern for these two main aspects of bilingual- bicultural programmes, which they consider most relevant in evaluating their implications for both the child and his/her community. On the one hand their studies attempt to investigate the role of L1 in the curriculum (how, to what extent, and for what objectives it is taught); on the other, their examinations focus on the impact of minority language maintenance on the wide socio-cultural context. Within this perspective, which integrates the linguistic and social goals at the levels of both the individual child and the minority community, the school curriculum has become the focus of discussions concerned with the evaluation of different programmes. On the one side, the system of alternation/switch of the two media of instruction has been seen as the major factor responsible for the development of the child's language competence; on the other, the question of what subject should be taught in what language - and especially how the minority culture component should be incorporated in teaching syllabuses and materials - have been considered to be crucial in evaluating the programmes' long-term impact on the community language as well as in determining whether they were genuinely bicultural as well as bilingual.

In reference to the impact of the bilingual curriculum on the minority child's linguistic and cognitive development, some scholars, such as Swain and Cummins among others, have extensively investigated questions relating early bilingualism to cognitive functioning and the optimum age for L1-L2 switch and attainment in bilingual oral and literacy skills. Others, like Lambert, have discussed matters of bilinguals' cognitive achievement in relation to social and psychological attitudes of children in schools and parents in the community. Finally, others such as Toukomaa and Skutnabb-Kangas have concentrated on the relationship between the school curriculum for the minority child leading to certain levels of mono/bilingual abilities and cognitive development and the standards of scholastic achievment demanded by the majority groups to attain linguistic and social emancipation.

Regarding the impact of the bilingual curriculum on the minority community and its long-term implications for the overall socio-cultural context, scholars like Fishman, Spolsky, Kjolset, Paulston and MacKay, among others, have focused on the role of the minority language and culture in the school and the community which it serves, and have devised typologies to evaluate the cultural/-linguistic objectives of different programmes against the expectations of the minority groups concerned.

Works and discussions on such questions have been surveyed in three recent works (Swain and Cummins, 1979; Tosi, 1979b; Tosi, 1982) and will not be re-examined in this paper. It is, however, important to point out that in the extensive investigations on the several social, linguistic and educational factors, leading to different levels of success in bilingual/ bicultural programmes, little discussion has dealt with two aspects of paramount importance: the first concerns the cultural background, language competence and educational training of teachers; the second involves the criteria for planning the linguistic texture and the organisation of the cultural content of Ll reading and instructional materials. This paper is concerned in particular with the second aspect, although it is assumed that the criteria concerning the planning, design and evaluation of materials are also of crucial importance for identifying the content and objectives of training programmes.

It is notable that the papers and reports describing the criteria and use of materials adopted for mother-tongue teaching available thus far show predominantly the practitioners' concern to fulfill their immediate task in the classroom. This approach, though in some instances it might lead to very successful teaching, is not, however, a guarantee per se that the complex of linguistic factors characteristic of the special process of mother-tongue teaching in the context of second language learning, has been taken into account. The danger of any such empirical, non-systematic approach could be twofold. On the one hand, teachers who are not theoretically equipped to appreciate the peculiar mechanism of their pupils' learning process as different from other processes of language learning in different socio-linguistic and environmental conditions, might be led to conform their strategies and instruments to their perhaps more familiar experience of mother-tongue development or second language teaching. On the other hand, instruments for Ll teaching in some bilingual programmes, patterned on specific objectives and pupils' background, could inspire other mother-tongue teachers: these might resort to such materials, borrow, adapt or translate them, while in fact they may bear little relevance to the learning conditions of their own pupils. Experience has shown that this may be the case with teachers who have been trained as mother-tongue teachers in the homeland (i.e. teachers of Portuguese, Spanish, Italian and Turkish) as well as those who have been trained as teachers of general subjects or second language in the 'host' country (i.e. teachers from ex-colonial territories who are native speakers of those languages but were trained and qualified in the new country).

Although it is important to acknowledge that in language teaching, as in the teaching of other subjects, extensive research has shown that the method is less important than the teacher's competence, which in turn depends on the teacher's belief and confidence in what he/she is doing (CILT, 1969, cited in Wilking, 1972.), it is also important to remember that instructional and reading materials always have been considered factors of paramount importance for the success of any language learning programme. Naturally, these appear to be even more important when the teacher, who has been trained to cope with problems of a specific learning process, is faced with problems inherent in different learning conditions for which neither his training nor the instruments available have been specifically designed.

Theoretical framework

This paper attempts to offer a contribution towards the formulation of a model for the planning, design and perhaps evaluation of L1 instructional materials for bilingual/bicultural education and mother-tongue teaching programmes. In particular it aims to map all possible factors relevant to the learner, the target language and the environmental learning conditions, within the specific process of mother-tongue development in the context of second language learning.

Not all socio-linguistic factors concerning the child's background and speech community or all the linguistic structural pecularities pertaining to a language system here described will be equally, if at all, relevant in the case of instructional materials for all minority groups, their language programmes, syllabuses and objec- tives. At this stage, in fact, our aim is to make the model as uni- versally applicable as possible, rather than to demonstrate special concern for specific factors relative to particular situations.

It is possible that in the context of some bilingual education programmes, the consideration of factors relative to the distance between the 'dialect' or 'variety' spoken by the learner at home and the standard language of literacy used and taught in the classroom may be irrelevant. Also, where the minority community has recently arrived, and/or has achieved through favourable conditions of envi- ronmental exposure a high level of language maintenance avoiding phenomena of contact varieties, preoccupations concerning the standardisation of the spoken language to provide easier access to literacy, are obviously reduced. Both situations seem to be characteristic, for example, of the diglossic conditions of Finnish communities in Sweden as described by Skutnabb-Kangas and Toukomaa

(1980), who seem to have gained extraordinary benefit from the programme providing early reinforcement and literacy in the mother tongue later affecting performance in L2 oral skills and literacy.

This, however, is just an example; other programmes might have to face difficult and unusual technical problems in the development of materials relevant to early reading, literacy and cognitive activities. This might depend, for instance, on the need to invent a practical orthography for minority languages which were usually transmitted only via oral communication, as in the case of bilingual education in the Navajo reservations, as described by Spolsky (1974) and Holm (1975). Other difficulties might derive from the adaptation of a Roman or even non-Roman writing system of the minority language in order to make possible the transcription of the sound of some vocabulary of the majority language incorporated via phenomena of contacts, as in the case of initial literacy in Punjabi teaching within English schools described by Russell (1980). Other types of difficulty might arise when the minority language has undergone a mature process of assimilation in the new linguistic environment, and has developed substantial phenomena of interferences and contacts (viz. the cases cited in Brent-Palmer, 1979) due to poor sources of exposure and language infrastructure. Other and different questions may arise when the teacher needs to revive and develop a low status variety of a national language (chicano v. espanol mexicano) as described in Hernandez-Chavez (1975), in transitional or maintenance programmes: and, indeed, even more problems are to be faced by teachers who wish to exploit their pupils' native competence in a rural idiom, so far removed from the standard that it might not provide immediate intelligibility to that language, the command of which, only, can provide access to reading materials and literacy. (See the case of 'campano' speakers in classes of Standard Italian described in Tosi, 1979a and Tosi, forthcoming.)

In such a complex mosaic of diverse learning situations, one encounters different children's linguistic backgrounds, different programme objectives, different features of the sound and writing systems of minority languages, different distances between the spoken varieties and the standard languages of instruction and literacy, different degrees of intensity to environmental exposure and language infrastructures, and different communities' cultural and linguistic orientations and aspirations. It is not realistic, therefore, to expect that a model for the identification of the criteria for mother-tongue teaching materials could offer a body of practical guidelines for the immediate producion of appropriate syllabuses and instruments; rather, it can only suggest a guide for the teacher to perceive and to interpret a number of factors relevant to the specific circumstances of his/her programme. This paper should read as a contribution towards the conceptualisation of a framework for the identification and examination of the several sets of variables relevant to the construction of L1 teaching materials in a bilingual programme, either incorporated in the curriculum or even administratively disengaged from it.

Definition of the learning process

In the previous section it was pointed out that some characteristics of the pupil's learning process in developing skills and literacy in the minority language may be typical neither of first language acquisition nor of second language learning. In the following sections we will attempt to investigate the characteristics inherent in such a process - which we have proposed to call 'mother-tongue development in the context of second language learning' - and to analyse their implications in the planning and design of relevant teaching instruments. Before dealing with these tasks, however, we propose to represent visually the interconnection of the variables characteristic of this particular learning process in an integrated structure; and in order to clarify this structure, comparison will be made with other structures representing, respectively:

(1) monolingual development for monolingual children
(2) bilingual development for mono/bilingual children
(3) monolingual development for bi-dialectical children
(4) mother-tongue development in the contxt of second language learning.

An ideal model describing a language learning process is probably easiest thought of as similar to a multi-tiered cylinder. The bottom layer contains variables relative to the language spoken in the home and the immediate family environment; the middle layer contains factors relative to language infrastructure and sources of exposure in

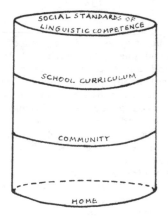

Fig. 1

51

the community; the top layer contains components characteristic of the school curriculum, as designed to develop its pupils' linguistic resources to meet the standards of language competence demanded by the society. The dimension of such standards is represented by the size of the top circle of the cylinder. Since the goal of any linguistic education policy is the achievement of these standards, it is clear that the greater the fulfilment of the volume of each of the three layers sustaining the top, the firmer the support given to the child's language development towards achieving those objectives.

The four different learning processes mentioned above can be visualised in the four cylinders below associated in three cases with other shapes representing the different distributions of variables relevant to different monlingual and bilingual learning processes.

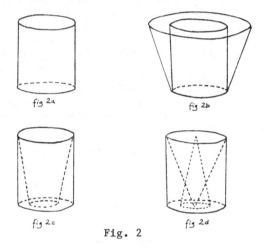

fig 2a

fig 2b

fig 2c

fig 2d

Fig. 2

Fig. 2a represents the typical situation of monolingual children from a family background where the standard language is spoken, and linguistic guidance and support is provided by the parents and the immediate circle of neighbours and peers. Also they are exposed to the same language in an environment rich in sources of exposure to selected and sophisticated patterns of linguistic interaction. The school's role is concerned in reinforcing and organising their language competence to meet the demands of the curriculum. Their overall monolingual development in the standard language is protected and directed towards the achievement of the standards demanded by their monolingual school and society; standards that they are most likely to meet as a result of concomitant situations converging their language development into a channel (the cylinder) which concentrates their efforts to the fulfilment, without dispersions, of the academic and social goal set in that society.

Fig. 2b represents the even more uncommon, and privileged, situation of bilingual development for children from a solid mono/bilingual background, who benefit from educational provision aiming to bilingualism in a high status foreign/second language. The figure consists in a cylinder corresponding to the situation described in the previous section where the base may or may not include a bilingual situation at home. Whilst the same measures are taken to secure a solid linguistic development in the home, school and community main language, others are also introduced to expand this child's academic and social opportunities. The volume enclosed between the cylinder and the truncated cone surrounding it, represents at level of family, community and school curriculum, the extra measures taken within the three adjoining sections to maintain and develop a bilingualism at no detriment to a solid linguistic experience and education in the mother tongue. While the linguistic standards demanded by the society in one national/standard language – also the pupil's mother tongue – are achieved (top circle), also the chances for enriching bilingualism in another high-status language are increased (as represented by the wider circle of the truncated cone), together with the chances to be able to operate linguistically in a multi/inter/national dimension.

Fig. 2c represents the far more common situation of monolingual schooling for a child who lives in a bidialectical family and environment. The standards of linguistic competence demanded by society in the national language remain the same, as represented by the top circle, whilst the truncated cone enclosed in the cylinder represents the limited family/environmental support available to the child for the development of his/her competence in the standard language. In particular, a limited family training in the Standard, poor sources of exposure to that language in the community, the inability of the school to cope effectively with bidialectism (often resting on the principle that equal treatment means equal opportunities) – all these result in a dispersion of efforts (represented in Fig 2c by the section of volume between the cylinder and the truncated cone). This happens when the school and society only value competence in the Standard and disregard or even penalise any other dialect.

Fig. 2d represents the process identified as 'mother-tongue develop-ment in the context of second language learning', one typical of minority pupils learning their first language in an immigrants' society. The top circle representing the standards of linguistic competence necessary to achieve equal social opportunities typically remains the same in a society with a multilingual population – but a monolingual policy – as in a society with a monolingual population (compare Fig. 2a). The achievement of such standards, however, becomes even more difficult for the linguistically diverse children, than in the situation described in Fig. 2c. In fact, their point of departure – the family support in relation to the majority's (L2) language – tend to be nil (which in the figure is represented by the apex of the inverted cone). Facilities for L2 development progressively increase in the environment and the school, although they tend to form a much poorer complex of environmental situations in comparison to those in the three other cases. The mother tongue, instead, starts from a more favourable position – as represented by the base of the other cone – although often it might be a rural or contact dialect of little use outside the community and stigmatised even in the homeland. Its development might originally benefit from rich intrastructure within the family and neighbourhood, but in later life, not reinforced by full conditions of exposure, the mother tongue might develop only within restricted domains. At school, with the exception of those countries which have adopted a bilingual education policy, the mother tongue might occupy a minimal portion of the timetable or even be confined outside the monolingual school. Overall, time and resources to develop linguistic and academic skills in the mother tongue can be just as limited as the inclination of the majority society to maintain and value bilingualism in minority communities. The volume which represents the constraints of mother-tongue development in the context of second language learning (the latter component represented by the cone in the inverted position) tends to take the shape of a cone with the apex in the area of social demands for linguistic competence; at that level competence in the minority language can be considered quite irrelevant with regard to social opportunities, and the society's appreciation for bilingualism tends to shrink to become a small point in those countries which neither value nor encourage qualifications for literacy in minority languages.

A comparison between the two shapes representing two situations of bilingual development, one including a form of bilingualism valued and the other one disdained by the society, shows that in the first case the original cylinder is embraced by additional volume, as in Fig. 2b, whilst in the other cylinder (Fig. 2d) a portion of volume has been subtracted. This accords with Lambert's (1977) distinction between 'additive' and 'subtractive' bilingualism. He says that in the first situation 'the bilingual is adding another socially relevant language to his repertoire of skills at no cost to his L1 competence'; in the second, 'the bilingual's competence in his two languages at any point is likely to reflect some stage in the 'subtraction' of L1 and its replacement by L2'. The latter case, Lambert further comments, is typical 'of many ethnic minority groups who, because of national educational policies and social pressures of various sorts, are forced to put aside their ethnic language for a national language'. As these speakers may be characterised by less than native-like competence in both languages, some recent studies have discussed their conditions in terms of 'double-semilingualism' or 'semilingualism' (on this notion see the survey articles by Swain and Cummins, 1979; and Tosi, 1982).

PLANNING LEVEL: CRITERIA FOR THE COURSE

The language

Mother-tongue development in the context of second language learning only refers to particular conditions which characterise a learning mechanism from others. Having identified, theoretically, this process, little can be said to specify qualities and features of the process unless we refer, in practice, to the two systems of the languages concerned. In particular, this paper is concerned with the learning of English as a second language and with minority languages spoken in ethnic communities of English speaking societies. It is important, for the EMT and ESL teacher to realise that the particular principles, strategies and practices that have formed his/her teaching training, are closely related to the particular learning processes involved in the acquisition of the mother tongue, or the second language as well as the particular features of the target language, i.e. English. It is equally important for minority language teachers acting in a mother-tongue class to realise that the particular characteristics involved in their pupils' learning process, depend not only on the constraints of their linguistic background, but also on the particular features of the minority language involved. Teachers must bear this in mind, especially when engaging in drawing reading schemes, preparing syllabuses and grading instructional and reading materials. They may resort to their native competence and their training and experience and apply the latter two for the best exploitation of the former. This might not always work satisfactorily. The teachers who are most likely to encounter difficulties, or indeed introduce them unintentionally, are the minority teachers, native speakers of an ethnic language, who have been trained in the host country. Unless their training contained a strong element of descriptive and applied linguistics, they may transpose theories relevant to the reading of English to other language sytems and they may assume that skills required to translate graphic symbols into spoken language units are the same irrespective of the language system with which they are dealing. But also minority teachers trained in their country of origin to teach mother tongue in the homeland are likely to feel uneasy when using criteria, strategies and materials with pupils whose linguistic background does not match with their expectations. However, they may be more aware of the inadequacy of their training, simply because they are already familiar with the criteria which co-ordinate materials, methods and procedures with the special requirements of the learners of that language. Once these requirements have changes (i.e. pupils' linguistic background, environmental conditions) they feel that both their training and materials are inadequate: in particular, they are able to point out that the criteria behind the co-ordination between reading materials, methods and procedures need to be revisited to suit the different level of the learner's 'mother tongue' competence.

The literature available on the relationship between the symbol-sound correspondence in difference language systems and the teaching of reading shows that crucial differences in the way writing represents speech pose completely different problems to early readers in different languages. Although the dichotomy between the segmented and global view of learning to read continues to persist – and it is unlikely that it can substantially influence future design of instructional and early reading materials – the actual teaching of reading, in contrast with discussions on the learning process, should not be segmented into exclusive sub-skills training. However, for the task of designing relevant teaching materials, the consideration of the particular features of a language is of crucial importance in that they affect the learner's skills involved in decoding both the symbol and the message. For this practical purpose it is important for teachers and material producers to examine the complexity of the symbol-sound relationship at two separate levels: the identification of the symbol and the interpretation of the message. This is not to say that the early reader operates the two skills independently, nor that they should be separated for the purpose of teaching; simply, it helps to clarify how different language systems present diverse problems to the child who is struggling in the early stages to identify the symbols set before him/her in order to translate them into language units.

Skills related to identification

features of the symbols	nature of the relationship between symbols and spoken form
- degree of complexity - degree of discriminability - degree of visibility - degree of constancy	- degree of consistency (variations of sounds are presented by single letters or combinations) - degree of constancy (letters/combinations can be read invariably in only one way).

Skills related to interpretation

- vocabulary   - syntactic structures   - content
1) complexity of sentence construction   3) cultural relevance
2) relationship between spoken/written code   4) domain specific

Fig. 3

If the skills related to interpretation of the message depend
largely on the complexity of the linguistic texture of the text and
its content - factors relevant especially to the learner's oral
competence and linguistic background (i.e. complexity of sentence
construction, relationship between spoken/written code, cultural
relevance, domain specificity) - the skills related to the
identification of the symbols depend specifically on the features of
a particular language system. Accordingly, the relative ease or
difficulty of the learner's task will be largely influenced by the
particular features of the written symbols that s/he has to deal
with as well as by the nature of their relationship with the spoken
language. As for the features of the symbols, languages vary
greatly according to four major qualities: complexity,
discriminability, visibility and constancy. The first quality
(<u>complexity</u>) refers to the degree of difficulty faced by the learner
when trying to identify the meaning of independent units. The
system of our Roman alphabet is relatively easy when compared with
an alphabet or an ideogram system including many serifs, curves,
dots, etc. <u>Discriminability</u> refers to the degree to which single
units of a system resemble one another; again, our Roman alphabet is
a relatively easy one when compared to others, yet as teachers of
languages written with the Roman alphabet know, early readers find
difficulties in telling 'b' and 'd' and 'p' and 'q' apart. Here the
case is not only that these letters closely resemble each other, but
also that they are identical except for orientation. <u>Visibility</u>
refers to the size of the graphic symbols used; in the Roman
alphabet, for example, they tend to be all of approximately the same
size, but in others, minute symbols can combine with larger ones,
modifying completely the phoneme which they represent. In Hebrew,
for example, a single dot can assume eight different functions
according to its location in relation to other graphemes. Finally,
<u>constancy</u> is the quality which refers to the relative unchangeabi-
lity of graphic symbols to represent the same language unit. An
example from the Roman alphabet is the varying printed forms in
which letters such as 'a' and 'g' occur in English; another is the
different form of writing 'r' in English (r) and other European
languages also written in the same alphabet (*?). But examples of
more complex cases can be drawn from other languages where the same
phonemes are represented by different letters depending on their
position in the word. In Arabic, for example, the same symbol takes
a different form whether it appears at the beginning, the middle, or
at the end of the word.

These four qualities relating to the features of the symbols in
writing systems concern particularly languages written in a
non-Roman alphabet and they are likely to present some special
problems concerning the design of reading schemes as well as the
preparation and grading of materials. But qualities describing the
special features of the graphic symbols used in a language are not
the only ways in which written language systems differ from one

another. Equally important is the nature of the relationship betwen symbols and sound; some languages are commonly referred to as 'highly phonetic' and others as considerably less so. This quality describing the degree to which a phonetic system is closely represented by the alphabet, depends on two factors: consistency and constancy. The degree of <u>consistency</u> is given by the same proportion of units or combinations of units of the same sound in a given language, which can be reproduced by different symbols. An example from English is provided by the sound /s/, which is differently represented in a word like 'circle' (with c) and 'sale' (with s). The degree of <u>constancy</u> is given by the frequency of some letters (or combinations of letters) which can represent different sounds. An example from English is the combination 'ea' which can be read in three different way in words such as 'eat', 'great', 'threat'. English is a language of both low consistency and low constancy, qualities which have considerable bearing on the development of early literacy reading and instructional materials. The same difficulties might not be encountered by producers of syllabuses and materials for other languages.

Take, for example, a language like Italian, with the same alphabet, and Greek, with a different alphabet: since both show high degrees of constancy and consistency, learning to decode is relatively easy. One of the important implications, at the level of planning bilingual reading schemes and evaluating the progress of the literacy skills in the two languages, is that for languages with high regular symbol—sound correspondence it is possible for the early readers to read fluently and correctly pages from a difficult text without understanding what they read – something which is not possible for early readers in English and other languages with a less regular symbol—sound correspondence. Another important implication of the different degrees of correspondence between symbol and sound in a language concerns the way in which the early reader might set about interpreting the graphic symbols. When in an early stage the reader attempts to derive the meaning word by word, does the meaning of each word come to their minds as a by-product of their being able to sound it correctly? Or, vice versa, during their attempt at identification, must the meaning of a word be understood before the reader can pronounce it? Most experienced teachers of English would maintain – and probably correctly so – that early readers of English are more often first aware of the meaning of a word and are only then able to sound it correctly. But this is not the case for readers of all languages, of Italian for instance, and others characterised by a highly regular symbol—sound correspondence: early readers of these languages will understand many words as a direct result of being able to sound them correctly.

These reflections on the features of different alphabets and the diverse degrees of correspondence between symbols and sounds – no more than an exemplification of the variety of factors underlying the different rationales for the construction of reading material — have concentrated specifically on questions inherent to the different writing systems. But they are not the only question with which the materials producers should concern themselves. Certainly this is not to suggest that the process of language learning and learning to read in particular is a transmission of a hierarchical order of skills which could only be described and developed by means of a linguistic approach. Thus identifying theoretically the process involved in the reading of a language does not imply that linguists alone can offer the optimal methodology and instruments to develop the relative skills. However, their contribution becomes relevant for the insight they can provide concerning the relationship between the features of a language and the appropriate teaching and testing instruments. Tests of oral proficiency and reading skills make little sense once translated into another language; likewise, the mere translation of words, sentences and passages from a reading scheme designed for one language into another might be of little relevance, and may indeed misrepresent the difficulties of the text and mislead the learners. This is a danger which experienced and competent teachers should be able to avoid when 'adapting' materials from one language for use in another: they must be able to distinguish between general educational principles and procedures for language pedagogy and the specific criteria especially devised best to represent and teach individual languages and their writing systems.

The curriculum

The preceding sections have considered how individual and environmental conditions make mother-tongue developments in the context of second language acquisition a learning process different from others; and also why the particular features and relationship between sound and writing systems may involve special skills and difficulties in the mechanism of learning to read in a given language. In this section the analysis will concentrate, particularly, on the teacher's need to appreciate the circumstances of the "mother tongue curriculum" as distinct from the monolingual EL1, the ESL, and the FL curricula.

School attitudes towards teaching minority languages may range from outright prohibition to neutrality; in more positive situations, schools may agree to promote them in a number of ways, from a midpoint of permissiveness to a point where they are used as media of instruction. The table below summarises, from negative to positive, educational practices and attitudes towards the use of the mother tongue at home and at school.

Attitudes Regarding Use of the Mother Tongue

	Negative		Neutral	Positive	
				Taught to host group	Used as a medium of instruction
At school	Prohibited : : :	Ignored : : :	Permitted : : :	: : :	: : :
		: : Riduculed		: : Used by teachers	: : Taken to literacy
At home	Discouraged ——————————		Ignored —————		Encouraged

Fig. 4   (from Krear, 1969)

As for the position and role of the mother tongue in the curriculum, two main aspects of programmes have been identified by researchers as most relevant when evaluating their implications for both child and community. One involves the role of the minority language in the curriculum: how, to what extent, and for what objectives it is taught. The other focuses on the impact of minority language maintenance in the overall socio-cultural context, i.e. assimilation or pluralism. Accordingly, scholars of bilingual education have devised models grouping the different programmes into categories. Most of them seem to agree that there can be two major orientations in such programmes:

Compensatory/transitional. The L1 is used to enable the poor/non-speaker of the L2 to master subjects until skills in L2 are developed. The outcome is transitional bilingualism for the child and assimilation for the minority group.

Language Maintenance. The minority language is emphasised and introduced as a more stable medium of instruction, while the L2 is introduced gradually, until they both become media of instruction for all subjects. The outcome is balanced- bilingual-coordinate competence in individuals, and cultural pluralism in the community. The minority group preserves its own language and becomes diglossic for compartmentalised intragroup and intergroup purposes.

These two models clearly refer to educational contexts where the school has already developed organisational and curriculum flexibility to incorporate more than one language as a vehicle of instruction. In particular they refer to programmes of bilingual education in the US, Canada, and Sweden. However, they might be less significant in the school context of most European countries, and in particular Britain, where mother-tongue teaching is presently being discussed in terms of <u>whether</u> and <u>how</u> it should be incorporated in the curriculum rather than for what timetable, duration and subjects it should be integrated into a bilingual curriculum.

The following diagram attempts to summarise some of the major patterns of mother-tongue teaching in programmes either developed by the school in the curriculum, or "hosted" by its authorities in areas inside or adjoining the curriculum, or even in programmes detached from the school both physically and in relation to content.

MODELS

5.1 L_1 reinforcement

5.2 $L_1 - L_2$ equal weight

5.3 L_1 curricular subject

5.4 L_1 subject adjoining
        the curriculum

5.5 L_1 subject separate from
        the curriculum

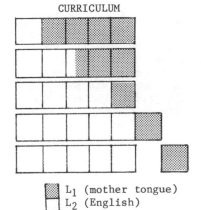

CURRICULUM

L_1 (mother tongue)
L_2 (English)

Fig. 5

In the table above every row corresponds to different positions of the mother-tongue programmes in relation to the curriculum. The different curricular programmes, in order to make them significant to the British situation, have been divided into 5 equal squares corresponding to the number of periods of a school day as well as the number of school days per week. Each square, therefore, corresponds to 1/5 of the whole curriculum, and may be taken either as a portion of the day timetable or as a portion of the week timetable.

The first model (Fig. 5.1) is firmly integrated in the curriculum. It obviously involves the use of the mother tongue for the teaching of other subjects in order to cover the different curricular areas. To this model belong both programmes beginning with the sole use of the mother tongue as well as those adopting it while leaving a small portion of the timetable for the teaching in, or of, the second language. The aim of these programmes is reinforcement of Ll oral skills and literacy before the introduction of literacy in the second language. However, they diversify themselves later according to whether they maintain and promote both Ll and L2 as stable media of instruction (maintenance programmes), or they simply aim to reinforce Ll to enable pupils to develop cognitive abilities and master subjects until skills in L2 are completely developed (transitional programmes). In Britain examples of neither of these two programmes can be found, while the first corresponds typically to the provision described by Skutnabb-Kangas and Toukomaa in their report (1976; see also Toukomaa and Skutnabb-Kangas, 1977), the second corresponds to some Canadian programmes as well as many of those set up in the US within the Bilingual Education Act.

The second model (Fig. 5.2) is also built into the curriculum and the mother tongue is used as a point of departure, but only for a portion of the timetable corresponding to half of the school curriculum, or less. After a short period - a few terms of 'adjustment' - the role of the mother tongue as a vehicle of instruction may decrease to the point of disappearance after one or two years. As the principal aim of this model is bridging the linguistic mismatch between the country of origin (or the home) and the school - and in the long term seeks fluency and literacy only in the L2 - competence in the Ll may ultimately be unimportant in the child's overall scholastic and academic development, and literacy in that language might not even be sought. When this is the case, the nature and objective of the programme remains strictly compensatory. A programme which falls somewhere within this category is the Bradford MOTET project.

The third model (Fig. 5.3) also includes a mother-tongue component in the curriculum, but it differs from the previous programmes in that the learners' bilingual state is neither taken into account as a resource to develop (5.1) nor as an obstacle to monolingual education (5.2) which is to be overcome. The mother tongue is offered as a school subject (alternative to another course of the modern language curriculum) at secondary level, or as an option available in occasional withdrawal classes at primary level. In both cases the timetable constraints would impose limits on the use of the mother tongue to teach other subjects. Some courses may claim to do this with classes on 'language and culture' or 'language and social studies', while limitations of time effectively prevent using that medium for activities other than the reinforcement of linguistic skills. Yet in this type of programme, a crucial difference exists between (a) those planned to offer a continuum from primary to secondary schools, based on a stable policy implemented throughout the community settlement; (b) the isolated courses in the secondary curriculum introducing literacy to pupils with no previous formal instruction (and therefore subject to a high degree of L2 dominance); and (c) primary withdrawal classes which do not even offer a guarantee of continuation or academic reward in the secondary curriculum. The latter two (b and c) typically describe the constraints and limitations of 'pilot projects' and other 'experimental schemes' such as the 1976-1980 Bedford programme.

In the fourth model (Fig. 5.4), mother-tongue classes are offered outside the school curriculum, taught by external instructors and financed, administered and supervised by non-statutory bodies. They may be incorporated in the school physically, but outside the normal timetable – during lunch, playtime or 'club' hours – and not always co-ordinated to its curricular and pedagogical contents and procedures. Some of these programmes may receive financial help and be subject to educational control from the country of origin; other from private agencies in the 'host' country. The instructors might be operating on a purely voluntary basis, or receive outside assistance from voluntary organisations. Some might actually be staff in the same school which employs them to teach other subjects, and probably begin their course on their own initiative although with the support of the Head and colleagues. Others may simply be sent by the country of origin, protected by an agreement stipulated by the two national authorities, and encouraged to make an impact in the local school, which may feel that it has little to say about the scheme. Other instructors might just be using the school as one of the many letting centres in town, providing space for any social/-leisure evening activity, and feel that there is neither connection nor channel of communication available with the school, as they are even prevented from using equipment and facilities other than its physical space. In all such programmes, the school's attitude towards the mother-tongue class and the influence on its curriculum may vary greatly: from an informal but co-operative co-management to an attitude of uncommitted sympathy or tolerance or even, in some cases, to total ignorance and indifference. The teachers relationship within the community school might be, at best, one of good support, although their own and their pupils' work are confined within the area of non-curricular activities; at worst it might be one of total frustration when the teacher is permitted to use the community school premises, but is excluded from its role and facilities.

In the fifth model (Fig. 5.5), the mother-tongue programme is separate even physically from the community school. This situation, while it may present little difference in terms of organisaton and facilities when compared with the last type of programme (described in model 5.4), may further widen the gap with the mainstream education: the physical conditions in which such programmes operate may misrepresent to the parents and to the school the educational goals of the mother-tongue teaching course. Certainly such conditions can cause the pupils to perceive and interpret them in antagonism, if not in conflict, with the objectives pursued by their day curriculum.

Programmes included in the first two models of the diagram (5.1 and 5.2) incorporate concern for the child's bilingual state and accept its significance in his/her linguistic cognitive and overall educational development, although with different degrees of emphasis in viewing it as a resource to exploit or a disadvantage to compensate for. The third model shows interest in the minority language, but while integrating it in the timetable as a subject, the course does not exploit it as a vehicle in cognitive areas of the curriculum: therefore it is not concerned with the co-ordination and assessment of the child's knowledge in the two languages comparatively. Finally, in the last two models even the structure (i.e. the school), within which the development and assessment of the child's bilingual abilities should be carried out, is missing. In these cases the chances to establish co-ordination between the principles and procedures for the teaching of that language are left up to the good will and personal efforts carried on between the minority language teachers and the staff of the mainstream school.

The relationship between the mother-tongue programme and the school curriculum presents a wide range of implications for the course and materials planner. At the level of pupil's involvement and motivation, the school attitude and co-operation can influence critically the scope and success of the programme. At the level of co-ordination of the learning, the school has the privilege, and the sole authority, to plan the implementation of co-ordinated syllabuses, materials and procedures for L1 and L2 teaching. At the level of resources, the school alone can determine whether and to what extent the minority language teacher may or may not use the equipment allocated by the authorities to serve the educational needs of its community. Finally at the level of materials planning, all the previous conditions of curriculum and resources become instrumental in the preparation of a syllabus containing realistic objectives matching, on the one side, the pupils' linguistic background, and on the other, the minority community's linguistic needs and cultural aspirations.

The objectives

There is little doubt that in times when economic situations tend to have an overriding role in determining educational policies, including mother-tongue teaching for immigrant children, policy-makers and administrators will tend to sympathise with certain educational innovations predominantly in view of their implications at the level of scholastic reward and marketable skills. In the case of programmes aiming to establish progressive social policies as well as programmes reflecting newly validated theories of better learning opportunities (i.e. bilingual education for multiculturalism and transitional bilingual education for more efficient monolingualism), substantial curricular reforms will involve the direct intervention of central and local authorities (see the models 5.1 and 5.2 in the previous section). However, where only minor changes to the curriculum are necessary, it seems realistic to expect that arguments concerning the academic reward and marketability of skills might have a powerful influence upon the attitudes of Heads and staff in relation to the desirability and feasibility of minority language programmes. It is, therefore, of paramount importance for the course-designer to identify specific linguistic objectives within the framework of the school language policy, whereby the term language policy in this context refers to provision offered by the school to meet its community social needs and cultural aspirations vis à vis the standards for language competence and qualifications demanded by the overall society.

Minority language programmes, from the viewpoint of their linguistic objectives and their relationship with those set for L2 development, can be grouped in three broad categories.

<u>Integrated model.</u> In this model the linguistic objectives are identified in close examination with the areas of the curriculum to cover which both linguistic skills and cognitive use of the minority language are instrumental. This model includes both (a) programmes in the minority language covering the whole or most of the curriculum until a certain age, after which it becomes a medium for certain subjects only (see the curricular model 5.1 in the previous section), and (b) programmes where the minority language is used to cover only part of the curriculum from the start, while the other is covered by the L2 (see curricular model 5.2).

For both types of programmes, given the same level of pupils' initial competence, the linguistic objectives will be determined by two major factors:

(1) At synchronic level what skills and what cognitive functions are required to cope with the learning activities of a determined portion of the curriculum;

(2) At diachronic level, at what age the minority language is abandoned and replaced by the second language.

Although all those programmes which employ the minority language as a vehicle of instruction require an integration of linguistic objects within the curriculum components, they may vary in relation to a) the different levels of linguistic skills and cognitive functions in the mother tongue within the area of more or less

'academic' curriculum activities, and b) the time of switch to the
L2 which could take place at pre-literacy, basic literacy, or
post-literacy level.

Supplementary model. In this model the linguistic objects are set
independently from their relevance to the different cognitive areas
of the curriculum. As the minority language course forms an independent part of the curriculum, or an independent unit outside it, the
level of achievement in verbal and cognitive skills in the mother
tongue is viewed as bearing no significance to the child's overall
academic development, except that it is evaluated as a subject per
se. In this case the school authorities and staff may tend to regard
the function of the course as supplementary to the normal curriculum, but at the same time they may be inclined to exercise some
pressure to orientate its organisation and the definition of its
objects towards existing patterns of traditional modern language
teaching in the secondary curriculum and foreign languages in the
elementary school (FLES). Naturally it will be for the mother-tongue
teachers and the course planners to take into account, and to discuss with the other school staff, different advantages as well as
disadvantages of a given minority language course: from questions of
the benefit of early literacy development at primary level, to
problems relating to the literary content of examination syllabuses
at secondary level, often based on a puristic use of the Standard
and penalising more commonly spoken non-standard varieties.

Informal model. If the linguistic objectives of programmes in the
integrated model are determined by the integration and systematic
planning of the instructional use of the two languages, and those in
the supplementary model are identified within the supplementary, but
separate, role attributed to a course incorporated or adjoining the
normal timetable, the informal model refers to those programmes
characterised by the absence of any specific linguistic objectives.
These can be found especially in classes run outside the curriculum
and particularly those which are separated both physically and in
relation to content from the school.

Lack of linguistic objectives, however, should be confused neither
with lack of educational or cultural goals, nor with purposeless or
ineffective language instruction. Some of these classes may teach
the minority language and/or use it as a medium of instruction for
other subjects, including culture and social studies of the homeland; others may preserve the language exclusively for religious
purposes. It has been pointed out that the more emphasis is placed
on non-directly educational purposes (i.e. religious, partriotic,
political), the less attention is likely to be paid to linguistic
aspects (Tosi, 1979b). Some of the course planners in these programmes may consider the linguistic aspects (i.e. grammatical accuracy,
vocabulary development, contact varieties, advanced literacy, style
and register diversity) unimportant for the purposes of their

but many others, who see their relevance in relation to the pupils' development of competence and confidence in their mother tongue – and to the chances of furthering their pride in its written use – may be seriously concerned with the need to equip pupils with the relevant skills, and, also, to achieve the standards required to examiners in institutional tests of language competence.

The identification of a set of graded objectives, which may concern either the area of language fluency in relation to functions, or that of language accuracy in relation to structures, may provide some useful and systematic criteria for the development of materials and the organisation of instruction, even if this is not necessarily oriented to proficiency, examinations, or even language competence per se.

Since secondary (supplementary) programmes in the curriculum will tend to orientate their syllabuses and linguistic objectives to approximate those required by public examinations, it is realistic to expect that even those adjoining the curriculum will gradually follow this pattern. As for those which are physically separated from the school, some planners might decide to take advantage of the experience developed by other programmes in reorganising syllabuses and materials in a more systematic way, and might draw from these models to redefine their linguistic objectives. Others, instead, emphasising the special cultural/religious goal of their classes, and less concerned with the question of competence and literacy, might just wish to retain the informal nature of their teaching. This dimension of the minority community's cultural aspirations is of crucial importance for the course planner and materials designer. Programmes may well pursue linguistic objectives in disharmony with the community social and cultural orientation, if the dimension of community relation is overlooked and its members' true linguistic aspirations are disregarded. Considerations about the place of literacy, the dominance of the Standard versus dialects, and the preference in adopting one script rather than another for a certain language, might have quite a different significance in the Western tradition's perception than in that of the ethnic minority group whose members speak that language. Minorities might view these questions from a perspective which is still more influenced by their cultural and religious heritage than by the social pressure of the new environment: this tends to stigmatise different aspects of language behaviour and to privilege, predominantly, marketable skills of language competence.

On the other hand, minority groups speaking a variety of the national language of their homeland – especially of European origin – might want to take advantage of the mother-tongue programme to introduce their children to literacy, particularly early literacy, in their national Standard in case of an eventual return to the homeland and their children's reintegration in that school system. In this case the main preoccupation of the programme would not be the mismatch between home and school, and its linguistic objective would have to be identified - depending on the distance between the dialect and the Standard - in terms of a process of transfer from the former to the latter. Other groups, which could be more definite about settling permanently, but at the same time are more determined to maintain their original culture and language - perhaps a dialect in a particular script significant to their religious tradition - may wish to revive that variety and use it as a vehicle to preserve their special heritage, thus exploiting it as an instrument of ethnic cohesion within their community. Literacy in that dialect, or in the national language of the homeland, might not be the immediate concern of this group; then the linguistic objectives of the programme should not attempt to impose upon pupils constraints derived from preoccupations with accuracy or standardisation, which should, in this case, be delayed for later inclusion in the secondary curriculum.

It is obviously impossible to identify for all minority groups a common core of linguistic objectives, particularly for the primary and other non-examined courses. Given that these languages have different significant in relation to their speakers' attitudes and aspirations as well as in relation to their different uses and functions in the community, overall society, and sometimes even within an international context of movement of labour, the ultimate responsibility lies with the course planners. As competent judges of the difficulties inherent to their language, and aware of the timetable allowance, they should conform the objectives of their syllabus to those areas of knowledge and functions which are mostly sought after and valued by their community. When confident, as members of that community themselves, that they have interpreted with justice its cultural and linguistic aspirations, they should turn to those factors which they, as professionals of language teaching, should take into account when combining objectives, procedures and instruments in the design of a realistic syllabus. Such factors concern the pupils' age group, their initial competence and the skills/subjects to develop in the mother-tongue programme.

STRUCTURING LEVEL: CRITERIA FOR THE MATERIALS

The age group

The relevance of these three factors (age group, initial competence, skills/subjects) to the definition of a viable syllabus cannot be investigated in isolation from the external constraints of the programme: the latter depend on the total amount of time allowed for the learning and its distribution. Since these constaints in turn determine the characteristics of the different curricular models (as explained in page 49) the above-mentioned factors will be discussed with reference to the different curricular organisation of programmes. In the 'integrated programmes' type involving the use of the mother tongue to teach curricular subjects (see page 64 the question of age group will pose problems of a completely different nature to those resulting from programmes planned as separate units from the rest of the curriculum, whether they be incorporated, adjoining (supplementary model) or separate from it (informal model).

As the first type of programmes are addressed to children whose home language differs from the language used by the school (either to maintain and develop competence and cognitive functions in L1 or to help children to master subjects until skills in L2 are developed) typically classes are offered from primary, or even nursery level. In this case factors relating to pupils' age might raise a wide range of questions concerning both the use of the language as well as the curricular content. Although an obvious temptation would be to draw from existing materials and syllabuses of programmes set up in the country of origin, these may include features that by their excessive ethnocentric orientation, the complexity of their linguistic texture and the general pedagogical approach, could not be immediately applicable to the curriculum in the new country. Other even more difficult problems might arise if the minority language used as a vehicle of instruction did not have an official status in the country of origin, or any other country, and were scarcely or never used for academic purposes; or if it were not used to cover in the same depth subjects and activities included in the bilingual curriculum. In some cases the two curricula (in the country of origin and the new country) may closely resemble each other in content and teaching procedures, as well as general educational approach for pupils of the same age; yet the linguistic texture of instructional and reading materials might prove unsuited to the learner's competence in the mother tongue in the foreign environment and would not match his/her cognitive abilities in that language. These factors, which depend on conditions of language infrastructure within the community, its use in the home and the intensity of exposure in the immediate environment will be discussed below under 'The learners initial competence'.

Quite different questions, directly relevant to the pupils' age, will have to be faced by the syllabus/material designer when planning for a programme of mother-tongue teaching as an independent unit, whether inside or outside the curriculum or peripheral to it. Compared with extra-curricular provisions, those programmes operating inside the curriculum naturally stand a far higher chance of developing materials reflecting particular subjects of interest to a specific age group, and co-ordinate their teaching procedures to those of L2; but their chances of grouping the pupils by age might not always be as high as outside the curriculum. The latter also might present difficulties of grouping by age, but their obstacles are more likely to depend on resources and organisation limitations, which are not always insuperable; whilst constraints affecting provision in the curriculum could be inherent to conditions of timetable, staffing and curriculum content which are often under the control of an authority outside rather than inside the school.

Constraints of time allowance and distribution might exert a considerable influence in the grouping of pupils. In the case of a school only moderately converted to 'mother-tongue teaching' or facing objective difficulties in organising its multilingual population in viable teaching gruops, solutions to problems of both time allowance and distribution may be determined by practical arrangements rather than pedagogical considerations.

In such situations the teacher might have to struggle with a mixed ability group or, indeed, with a wide range of ages, although both situations have been indicated as undesirable conditions of any language learning programme. In the latter case in particular, the teacher will clearly perceive that the optimal balance between informal learning opportunities and formal classroom teaching differs for younger and older learners. In the preparation of their syllabuses and materials, teachers should bear this in mind and devise classroom techniques flexible enough to suit different age groups. At the same time they should also attempt to create common situations of language practice related to specific functions where the native or near-native competence could be exploited across the age groups, thus making the learning of the language incidental to the task of communicating about topics of common interest. Furthermore, if literacy is envisaged to be a desirable objective for the older pupils, the teacher should not be discouraged by the presence of younger pupils in the same class. This may imply a diversification of techniques, procedures and instruments, as well as the teacher's ability to implement them. As for the question of optimal age and literacy, it is important to remember what language pedagogy has amply demonstrated: that for any age or ability group, the most desirable conditions of language learning are not to be found in strict separation of skills or prohibition of reading and writing in the early stages, but rather for any age, in a concentrated timetable, which is more productive and less difficult to organise, than very small amounts of time over several years.

The learner's initial competence

If we look at the criteria governing syllabuses and materials design for school language programmes, there is a totally different assumption made in the case of the learner's initial competence in second/foreign language teaching than is made in the case of teaching in the mother language. In the first case the learner's initial competence (i.e. competence prior to any form of instruction) is assumed as nil. In the second case it is referred to as 'native', which often tends to be taken as synonymous with 'total mastery'. In some cases, especially with pupils from overseas speaking creolised varieties of the Standard, their dialects may be taken into account in teaching, reading and testing materials designed for mother tongue acquisition. But normally, and especially when diversity exists within the same country, the assumption is always made that the child's initial competence in the target language of literacy and cognitive functions is that of a 'native speaker': it is often up to the teacher to find out the justice of this assessment and to take the necessary measures to bridge the gap between the child's dialect and the school language which, within some national contexts, may be as wide as that separating independent systems (see for the Italian situation Mioni and Arnuzzo-Lanszweert, 1979 and A L and G Lepschy, 1977).

The particular conditions affecting the use of the mother tongue in the foreign environment have substantial implications for the development of the child's competence and the extent of its command prior to formal instruction. In any project designed for the production of language teaching materials, it is realistic to account only for the major characteristics of individual learners within a certain age group. Nonetheless, the case of minority languages taught as 'mother tongues' in the context of second language learning, among the major characteristics there may well be included some other important factors. These concern:

(a) the distance between the language spoken in the home and that taught in the programme;
(b) the extent of its use in the household; and
(c) the degree of exposure in the community.

These conditions could be easily identified by the course/ material designers in a local project, but they could also display common basic patterns in different settlements at a national level, thus providing important guidelines for materials which could be relevant to the learners' abilities in programmes spread throughout the 'host' country.

The first factor concerns the distance between the language chosen for instruction and literacy, and the dialect/s spoken by the children at home. In the cases of some minority groups, competence in these dialects may not impede natural intelligibility of the standard or another privileged code chosen for instruction, and could only marginally decrease accuracy in relation to production skills. But in other cases, when the term dialect refers to idioms based on a system substantially different from that of the Standard/national language, more time, training and more sophisticated strategies might be required to produce oral intelligibility. Certainly this will delay the transfer of skills into the language of literacy, thus making the problem of its development much more than a question

71

of accuracy. In fact when basic norms are neither naturally reproduced nor recognised, the problem of reading and writing can hardly
be defined as one 'anchored in a native competence'; in consequence
the teacher's effort towards 'standardisation' will actually involve
an oral training differing substantially from any operation of
'standardisation' purely concerned with grammatical accuracy. The
extent to which these factors can be exploited by the course/mate-
rial designers depends on the degree of linguistic homogeneity of
the minority group in relation to its geographic distribution. If
many dialects of the same minority language are represented within
the same community, it may be difficult to combine procedures and,
by their approach certain techniques will have to reproduce those
typical of second language teaching. However, the course/material
designers will find that this is not the case, as dialectical variations depending on regional varieties spoken in the homeland are
often just 'transplanted' in the new country by phenomena of 'chain-
immigration'. This occurs especially in the case of European migrant
labour, but is not restricted to this continent. In these cases a
uniform approach based on a contrastive study of the system of the
language of literacy and that of the dialect actually spoken might
not just be 'enlightening' in that it enables us to understand
pupils' early reading processes and difficulties; it may actually
provide criteria for the design of the most economical and effective
procedures to develop accuracy and/or standardisation in both oral
and written production skills. (Tosi, 1979a.)

The other two factors relevant to the pupils' initial competence
(i.e. the extent of minority language use in the household and the
degree of exposure in the community) depend on the extent to which
the minority groups are assimilated into the foreign environment.
Normally these factors are interdependent and whilst the latter is
more significant for the language reinforcement of the older child,
the former has more direct relevance to the language development of
the younger.

Whilst investigating patterns of communication in the home, we might
find that the new generation's use of the mother tongue is confined
predominantly to passive use. Moreover, the limited date provided by
one generation for the succeeding generation's grammar-building
process might not always offer sufficiently consistent models, thus
weakening the child's control of accepted standards and correct
norms. Furthermore, lexical and syntactical borrowings affecting
the minority language in the family's use might lead to discontinu-
ous development of the child's vocabulary and restrict its repertoire to a limited range of domains. Naturally all such phenomena
of language dominance and interference may influence parental confidence in the minority language and affect their success in linguistic intervention and guidance with the children. Accurate descrip-
tions of such attitudes will show complex and varied mechanisms of
interaction in different households, in the same community, or even

within the same family (with older and younger children); the Linguistic Minority Project in Britain has been set up to investigate these particular aspects. However, the course/material designers who are familiar with their local community and aware of the major patterns of linguistic behaviour of their ethnic group will probably be able to investigate the major orientations of such phenomena. Since these depend on the level of linguistic assimilation in each individual family – which in turn derive from the duration of the group's settlement, its size and distribution – they often tend to be features common to the whole community rather than characteristics typical of an individual family. Therefore it can often be expected that phenomena of language assimilation particularly affecting the child's competence in the mother tongue prior to any form of instruction tend to follow regular rather than accidental patterns within the same age group. The major implications of this family condition could be profitably investigated by the materials designer, especially at the level of children's vocabulary, which often provides the main ingredient for most pre-literacy and early reading materials.

The third factor affecting the learner's initial competence involves the development of linguistic infrastructures within the minority community and the intensity of environmental exposure to that code adopted for literacy and instruction by the school. The development of language infrastructures refers to both formal as well as informal occasions of linguistic interactions between the adult members of the minority language group. In other words, it represents the degree of 'stabilisation' of diglossia within the minority group, which facilitates the development of individual co-ordinate bilingualism and thus avoids compartmentalisation of competence resulting in such phenomena as loss of vocabulary, confusion of registers etc. in the minority language. Within the network of linguistic infrastructures the conditions of exposure refer in particular to the institutional sources of language use. These are responsible for reinforcing abilities related to more 'formal' functions and also enhancing the status of the minority language; something which becomes important particularly at the level of community confidence. Community organisations, clubs, societies as well as libraries, newspapers, T.V. and radio programmes, and public notices, administrative and other official documents can have substantial influence on the first generation's desire to maintain their linguistic heritage, and on the second generation's ability to develop it. The existence and impact of these resources are not just important in avoiding cultural isolation, but are actually necessary to create those external conditions for language reinforcement without which the group would be condemned to 'concealed linguistic assimilation'. In particular for those groups who have developed bidialectism with the Standard, through social interaction and contacts rather than formal education or family background, favourable conditions of exposure and linguistic infrastructure have direct relevance in preventing a relapse into illiteracy and in avoiding phenomena of return to monodialectism.

73

Linguistic resources of this type in the neighbourhood are of great relevance for the course/materials designer, not merely because they supply the opportunities for actual language use and cultural interaction for the older pupils. They are also directly responsible for circulating reliable models among parents for the control of their own language, ultimately influencing their confidence and competence in exercising influential intervention in the younger pupils' language development in the home. In particular material designers should bear in mind that the extent of the influence of environmental sources of exposure on the child's initial competence may be significant to the course in many different ways. In the case of a minority language, developing in the new foreign environment contact phenomena with the majority language progressively accepted by the community in the minority's media and written language, the language maintenance programme should accept and incorporate this evolution. Whilst, in the case of a group whose first generation is compelled to return to the original village dialect by the lack of exposure to the Standard in the new country, it might not be appropriate to accept and reinforce in the instructional and reading material family models on which the new generation's initial competence is based. This is likely to be the case when a community, although it does not stigmatise its native dialect in the every-day use, nonetheless is more interested to use the mother-tongue programme to develop competence in the Standard, especially when this is the only medium of access to social emancipation and reintegration in the homeland, and the only language variety leading to examination awards and marketable qualifications in the new country.

The skills/subjects

It has already been pointed out that any course/material for a language teaching programme must allow for methodological flexibility in relation to the teacher's style as much as it should aim to incorporate those procedures that language pedagogy has shown to be the most effective for the different age groups. The criteria outlined in the previous sections of this paper intend neither to contradict these principles nor to challenge the practical guidance available in many useful works on language pedagogy for the younger and older pupils. Rather, they aim to contribute to the expansion of the theoretical considerations contained in those studies by introducing new ones particularly relevant to the sociolinguistic circumstances of minority language learning and to the specific conditions of a process of mother-tongue development in the context of second language acquisition. It is important, however, to remind the reader of the tentative nature of pilot studies like this and also to point out to school officials comparing the work of minority language teachers with the teaching of other languages or subjects (like French, mathematics or reading) that although these have been established in the curriculum much longer, they too have by no means solved all their problems.

One important implication of the previous discussion may be that while most programmes of foreign language teaching can realistically assume that their pupils' knowledge prior to instruction is nil, and whilst many of those of mother-tongue teaching only make sometimes dubious claims that their pupils' competence is 'native', in the teaching of the mother tongue in the context of second language learning it may range from one extreme to the other. It is only within the boundaries of a specific community, if not within those of a specific urban area, that the organisation of a programme, the design of its syllabus and the selection of appropriate material can make good sense. Accordingly, the definition of the programme objectives concerning both language skills and subjects to be taught through the medium of the minority language, should be studied in the context of the constraints of the curriculum, the time allowance and distribution, as well as the characteristics of the pupils' particular community in relation to both its level of language assimilation and its demand for language maintenance. In every programme the task of the material designer, or the teacher responsible for the selection of material, will greatly vary according to these factors: however, it should be expected that once some major problems of 'bilingual education' or 'mother-tongue teaching' programmes have been developed to fulfil specific educational goals, different curricular models and instruments will nevertheless be transferable from one school to another.

From the viewpoint of educational goals it is likely that programmes will divide into two major groups. <u>Programmes covering curricular concepts</u>. These will include programmes covering the whole or most of the curriculum for a varying period of time as well as those incorporating the teaching of one or two subjects only. Naturally all these programmes will need a special research component for the preparation of adequate teaching materials. Some minority languages may, in fact, not have the technical terminology or the suitable approach, or both, for the curriculum and certainly the problems of producing adequate reading and instructional texts cannot be overcome simply by producing accurate translations.

<u>Programmes teaching the language as a curricular (or extra curricular) subject</u>. Such programmes will obviously require substantially different materials, syllabuses and procedures whether they are planned to be part of the primary or secondary curriculum.

In particular programmes in the primary curriculum may be required to develop basic oral and literacy skills, following the patterns of some foreign language programmes for younger children (FLES). This may offer the best approach in the design of a course and preparation of its materials when the learners' initial competence is severely affected by his/her community's high degree of assimilation of the language of the new country; or when the learners' initial competence closely approximates to that of a native, but in a variety substantially different from the Standard language of instruction. In the latter case the material designer might be able to develop a methodology based on a 'transfer' approach; but should the community's linguistic background be heterogeneous in relation to different varieties, she/he will then prefer to go for the less ambitious approach predominantly based on the existing practices of teaching foreign languages to young children.

At primary level the situation is obviously different, should children be already fluent in the variety of the language for literacy and instruction. In this case syllabus and materials might profitably concentrate on the development of different areas of knowledge and skills through that language. Also the stages of literacy skills could be introduced at a rate closely approximating that of the pupils' major language of instruction. When this is the case, teachers/materials designers will find it very useful to develop contacts with other teachers in the school and plan their syllabuses and schemes of work in co-ordination with other curricular subjects and activities.

Language programmes functioning as independent courses inside, peripheral to or outside the secondary curriculum will also require different objectives and instruments in relation to the pupils' background. In some cases pupils might come to the secondary school from a primary programme which has successfully achieved fluency and literacy levels comparable to those of the major languages of instruction. Others may come from another programme which could only provide basic skills with poor fluency and no literacy. Others, finally, with no previous instruction in that language, may have maintained only a very poor level of decoding abilities predominantly tied to informal family communication: in this case the extent of L2 dominance on the L1 might effectively impede any functional use in the latter, thus reducing the process of learning it to a mechanism more typical of second language acquisition.

Such a variety of different learning situations is currently encountered among mother-tongue learners at secondary level. But the likelihood that such a complex situation will persist in the future, and that the education system, the local district, or even the individual school have to cater for such a wide ability range, naturally depends on the effectiveness of planning minority languages at the primary level. But even when policies are implemented uniformly from the primary level, the (secondary) school has to face for a number of years as long as the rationalisation of the system is completed, different constraints which lead to different types of practical objectives in the secondary programme. Materials designed for minority languages in the secondary curriculum will have to reflect carefully these linguistic objectives tailored to the age group as well as the initial competence. For, instance in England the linguistic background of Punjabi-speaking children, as a result

of broadly similar patterns of settlement and language use at home
and in the community, tends to be relatively homogeneous at the age
of five. But only five years later the gap between the levels of
fluency and literacy in the language among different pupils at the
age of enrolment in the secondary school, can be remarkably wide.
The reasons are to be traced not only to their individual experiences within the community, but, more important, to the different
types of provision available to them (mainly outside the curriculum)
during their primary schooling. An implication of this is that only
diversified syllabuses and reading and instructional materials can
meet pupils' different needs and abilities and maximise the effectiveness of the teaching. Accordingly, a course book, reading scheme
or other instructional instruments based on the identification of
the learner's initial skills and the specific objectives of the
programme would appear to make more sense and be more manageable by
the class teacher rather than the traditional criteria used for the
classical foreign languages (secondary French or 'O' level French or
French from eleven etc).

The cultural component

In the previous sections, which included a definition of the process
of mother-tongue development in the context of second language
learning, and a discussion of the relevance of its conditions and
mechanism in the selection of both the teaching approach and
materials, the criteria for the appropriateness of materials were
examined purely from a linguistic viewpoint. There is another
important aspect, however, that although often incorporated in the
areas of problems normally discussed by linguists, belongs equally
to fields investigated by other social scientists. This concerns the
cultural component of a language teaching programme, and in particular, in our case, specifically refers to the question of whether
minority language provision fosters biculturalism as well as
bilingualism, which means in less bureaucratic terms, whether it
aims to provide a more 'ethnocentric' or 'linguocentric' education.

For the purpose of this paper we have not adopted the approach of
other disciplines with a view to establishing how language materials
may incorporate concepts and contents oriented to one direction
rather than another, or whether one orientation is more desirable
for certain minority groups and less so for others. We are concerned
with underlining the fact that the task of the material designer is
not one which only concerns the professional linguist. Consequently,
unless the question of the cultural component is consciously faced
and answered, no linguistic work per se - however sophisticated it
may be - can guarantee that the materials produced actually promote
the cultural concepts which form part of the specific ethnic objectives that the programme aims to achieve. Even minority languages
programmes will have to deal with the question - like any other

language teaching programme – of _whether_ and _how_ the language course should provide pupils access to the related culture. Certainly this will imply that course and materials planners must achieve, in advance agreement on whether there are, and if so what are for the pupils, the educational advantages of maintaining the minority culture in a multi-ethnic school and society controlled by the majority group. On the other hand provision for minority languages could be planned with no special emphasis on the culture they embody. This 'linguocentric' orientation might be the option of members of a minority community wishing to identify themselves with the dominant culture. Such provision would still be in demand either to help the non/poor speakers of the majority/school language in the early stages, or even to preserve their language competence in more than one language as an individual and social resource. But should the maintenance of original traditions be among the aspirations of the minority group, and should they expect to make the most of the language programme to achieve it, the question of 'what cultural content?' might raise quite different problems in the teaching of minority languages than in that of traditional foreign languages.

Thus it becomes important to examine at what different levels a language can be presented in the process of teaching as a system embodying another culture, and in particular, how it can be operated as an instrument providing different degrees of access to and understanding and appreciation of that culture. What is said, read, narrated, or taught by the language teacher in the classroom can carry cultural meanings and connotations at two different levels: one relates to the language system and its use, the other to the corpus of attitudes, values and interests naturally associated with that language. Both areas include phenomena at micro- and macro-levels.

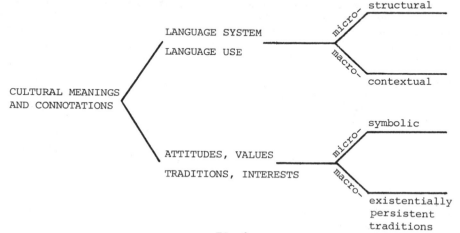

Fig.6

Phenomena of different cultural input could simply be conveyed by the system of the language itself or its use. At micro-level such phenomena consist typically in those concepts and meanings which belong to the cultural repertoire of a language and have no 'equivalent' words in another, so that they can be very poorly represented in translation. At macro-level they are found in the context of language use and although these phenomena do not concern equivalence of single meanings or divergent concepts within the two language systems, they result from traditionally different and irreconcilable patterns of behaviour and/or communication. Typically, this is the case of those foreigners in English-speaking countries who, on making new acquaintances, subsequently judge them indifferent to their welfare and brusque in personal relations because they have mistaken the customary greeting of 'How are you?' for a genuine enquiry about the visitor's state of health: they have then been disconcerted when their English-speaking acquaintances have not waited for a reply to the query (this example is taken from W Rivers, 1968).

Clearly, at these two levels cultural differences may emerge or even irrupt without any actual deliberate intervention on the part of the teachers to add to their instruction additional cultural elements. But a consideration of cultural means could also be planned to become part of the teaching programme and could actually be communicated in their association with the corpus of the values, traditions and interests of a different cultural group. However, it depends on the criteria adopted to identify this corpus in relation to the live cultural environment that programmes differ between the extreme of those emphasising micro-entities of 'symbolic ethnicity' and those emphasising macro-situations of 'existentially persistent traditions', in Kjolset's (1971) terms. In other words some programmes may decide to promote knowledge of some symbolic expressions of the minority cultural tradition, often stylised to suit the educational and vocational aspirations of the majority group, and quite possibly devised from a literary rather than oral and popular sources. On the other hand, others may wish to emphasise the more popular expressions of that culture to make them specifically relevant to its immediate users. Such programmes may also refer to the particular communicative/functional advantages of minority language maintenance, rather than supporting the privileges of literary education: in which case efforts will be concentrated on enhancing the status of the non-Standard variety as well as maintaining interests and values of the local community rather than promoting literary and institutionalised expressions of the national traditions from the country of origin. This preoccupation with the cultural and linguistic value of the local community traditions, as opposed to a more neutral 'linguocentric' education would characterise the course for a more 'ethnocentric' orientation.

Certainly a cultural component appears in any programme course and materials whether its educational goal tends to be predominantly 'linguocentric' and its social aim 'assimilationist' or whether they are both definitely 'ethnocentric'. But also it seems clear that in a programme 'linguocentric' in its aims and materials, the course planners could only claim to utilise its cultural component to point to cultural differences rather than cultivating and reinforcing them. On the other hand, if the programme aims to become an instrument to mitigate assimilation, it will need to plan and carefully operate the selection of those expressions which make its culture 'different'. If its materials only set out to emphasise its symbolic and prestigious expressions it might well fail to achieve its goal of offering palatable, useful and ultimately rewarding support for those cultural resources which are actually part of the community traditions.

* This paper is a compilation from material submitted to the Working Party on The Languages of Minority Communitites during 1981.

R E F E R E N C E S

BRENT-PALMER, C (1979). A sociolinguistic assessment of the notion "immigrant semilingualism" from a social conflict perspective. Working Papers on Bilingualism, no. 17, p 135–80.

CENTRE FOR INFORMATION ON LANGUAGE TEACHING (1969). Aims and techniques: language teaching methods and their comparative assessment; abridged proceedings of a conference held at State House, London WC1, on 20th and 21st March 1969. London: CILT for the Committee on Research and Development in Modern Languages. (CILT Reports and Papers 2.) p.30.

HERNANDEZ-CHAVEZ, E (1975). Consideraciones sociolinguisticas en materiales para la educacion bilingue. In: R C Troike and V N Modiano (q.v.).

HOLM, W (1975). The development of reading materials: the Rock Point (Navajo) experience. In: R C Troike and V N Modiano (q.v.).

KJOLSET, R (1971). Bilingual education programmes in United States: for assimilation or pluralism? In B Spolsky (ed) (1972): The language education of minority children. Rowley, Mass: Newbury House. p 94-121.

KREAR, S (1969). The role of the mother tongue at home and at school in the development of bilingualism. English Language Teaching, vol 24 no. I, p 1-4.

LAMBERT, W E (1977). The effect of bilingualism on the individual: cognitive and sociocultural consequences. In: P A Hornby (ed): Bilingualism: psychological, social and educational implications. New York: Academic Press. p 5-27.

LEPSCHY, A L and G Lepschy (1977). The Italian language today. London: Hutchinson.

MIONI, A and A M Arnuzzo-Lanszweert (1979). Sociolinguistics in Italy. International Journal of Sociology of Language, 21, p 81-107.

RIVERS, W M (1968). Teaching foreign-language skills. University of Chicago Press: Chicago and London.

RUSSEL, R (1980). An interview with A Sanghera on the teaching of Punjabi in Bedford schools, Urdu Teaching, 1, June 1980, p 1-4.

SKUTNAAB-KANGAS, T and P Toukomaa (1976). Teaching migrant children's mother tongue and learning the language of the host country in the context of the socio-cultural situation of the migrant family. Tampere, Finland. (Tutkimuksia Research Reports 15.)

SKUTNAAB-KANGAS, T and P Toukomaa (1980). Semilingualism and middle class bias: a reply to Cora Brent Palmer. Working Papers on Bilingualism 19, p 182-197.

SPOLSKY, B (1974). American Indian bilingual education. Albuquerque, New Mexico: University of New Mexico. (Navajo Reading Study Progress Report No. 24).

SWAIN, M and Cummins, J (1979). Bilingualism, cognitive functioning and education. Language Teaching & Linguistics: Abstracts, vol 12 no. 1, p 4-18.

TOSI, A (1979a). Bilinguismo, transfert e interferenze. Considerazioni sul processo di acquisizione dell'italiano in figli di emigrati bilingui in ineglese e dialetto campano. Paper from a conference on Linguistica Contrastiva, May 1979, convened by Societa di Linguistica Italiana, Asti. Forthcoming in Atti de Congresso.

TOSI, A (1979b). Mother tongue teaching for the children of migrants. Language Teaching & Linguistics: Abstracts, vol 12 no. 4, p 213-231.

TOSI, A (1982). Issues on immigrants bilingualism, "semilingualism" and education. AILA Bulletin I, 31.

TOSI, A (forthcoming). _Immigration and bilingual education_, Oxford: Pergamon Press.

TROIKE, R C and V N Modiano (eds). _Proceedings of the First Inter-American Conference on Bilingual Education._ Center for Applied Linguistics: Arlington, Virginia, 1975.

TOUKOMAA, P and T Skutnabb-Kangas (1977). _The intensive teaching of the mother tongue to migrant children of pre-school age._ Tampere, Finland. (Tukimuksia Research Reports 26.)

WILKINS, D A (1972). _Linguistics in language teaching._ Arnold: London.

TOWARDS A PROGRAMME OF IN-SERVICE TEACHER TRAINING FOR COMMUNITY LANGUAGE TEACHERS *

John Broadbent
Alperton High School, Brent

PERSPECTIVE

The presence of speakers of other languages than English in our schools has enriched our linguistic environment. The fact that from home to school they switch not merely between codes and dialects but between identifiably different languages means that any difficulties they experience in the schooling process may well assist in the drawing of general conclusions about the interaction of language and school learning.

There is still no proper overall provision for bilingual students, nor are the valuable language resources which they bring into our schools being promoted fully. Attempts to cater more adequately have tended to founder as a result of a shortage of properly trained and equipped bilingual teachers. Although in the long term the development of a satisfactory career structure for community language teachers is the only way to attract the requisite personnel, much can be achieved in the immediate term by establishing centres where bilingual teachers can develop their skills in the unique contexts created by the linguistic diversity existing in our English medium schools.

This paper attempts to offer some suggestions as to how existing branches of knowledge in the fields of teacher training, psychology and linguistics can be applied in the encouragement of community languages. Each individual school requires its own tailor-made language policy: in almost any U.K. school such a policy will be placed somewhere along a continuum between the provision of mother-tongue support for pupils whose second language is English, and provision for the learning of one or more community languages for those sections of the school population seeking additional linguistic and cognitive stimulation.

In this paper 'mother tongue' is taken to mean a language or dialect one learns to use in the home, whilst 'community languages' are those languages other than English which are used in the community/ cultural context. Other definitions and presuppositions in this paper are broadly equivalent to those used in the deliberations of the National Association for Multiracial Education (1981) Working Party on Mother Tongue and Minority Community Languages in Education, of which the present author was Chairperson.

COMMUNITY LANGUAGES AND CURRENT EDUCATIONAL THINKING

In 1982 when this paper was presented to the NCLE Assembly there were no teacher training institutions outside of Wales giving major attention to bilingual education. There were some university departments which specialised in the less commonly taught languages of Europe such as Greek, Italian, Polish, Portuguese, Spanish or Turkish, and others which dealt with Asian languages like Bengali, Chinese, Gujarati, Hindi, Punjabi or Urdu. A continuously updated list of courses available in such languages can be read in the Arts and Languages section of the Directory of Further Education published by CRAC: recent years have seen a continuous expansion in this area of language teaching. In some cases the Departments listed did take into account the variations from standard of the languages used by minority communities in Britain. None of them have as yet, however, succeeded in linking their areas of expertise with the major disciplines which underpin current educational practice, namely psychology, sociology and, increasingly, linguistics. In other words, not one of our existing educational establishments is creating a supply of teachers able to offer tuition in the languages of the ethnic minority communities. Nor did there seem to much in the way of facilities for enabling education psychologists, social workers, teachers and others to function through the medium of any language other than English.

In a perspective which views an education system in terms of a process capable of self-regeneration this state of affairs is extremely unfortunate. It has prevented the state system in Britain from providing the kind of education which future educators themselves are increasingly being shown to require. Without teachers trained to use the languages of minority communities in the UK it is simply not possible for LEAs to contribute directly, in the words of the 1944 Education Act, 'towards the spiritual, moral, mental, and physical development of the community by securing that efficient education throughout the stages shall be available to meet the needs of the population of their area'.

The Working Party which reported to the National Congress on Languages in Education (1980) on the various methodologies and materials involved in the teaching of English as a foreign language, modern languages and the mother tongue pointed out the importance 'in the converging work of EMT and ESL practitioners that the particular concerns of bilingual children are not forgotten. The current separation and different traditions of EMT and ESL do not easily allow the linguistic growth of bilingual children to be monitored and fostered as an integral part of the language teaching'.

A number of institutions for teacher education, particularly those who have come to adopt multicultural perspectives, do have the philosophical basis, the skills and indeed the willingness to service linguistic communities with the techniques and materials which can help them to enrich the educational background of the population as a whole. Of these, Birmingham Polytechnic, Moray House College of Education in Edinburgh, the Inner London Education Authority's Centre for Urban Education Studies, Middlesex Polytechnic, and St John's College of Further Education in Manchester will be offering during 1983–1984 pilot courses for an RSA Certificate in the Teaching of Community Languages. The Extramural Department of the School of Oriental and African Studies is also preparing to provide in-service support tailored to the specific needs of the Local Education Authorities who approach it for advice.

Continuing attempts to introduce into the maintained schools of the UK those languages which are used by distinct minority groups represent a logical and practical extension to the current debate on diversification in foreign language teaching, on linguistic diversity, on language across the curriculum, indeed, even on such seemingly tangential issues as study skills or criterion-referenced assessment of progress and on language across the curriculum. In a very short space of time these complementary concerns have begun to merge into a very considerable body of expertise which already exists in this country concerning education perspectives for a multiracial society. Delegates from the United Kingdon to symposia and seminars held b the Council of Europe at Donaueschlng in October 1981, and L, Aquila in May 1982 have been able to add constructively to the guidelines laid down by Porcher (1981) on preparing teachers to operate more positively in intercultural contexts.

Child-centrism

Successive reformulations of teaching objectives have based themselves on analysis of the effects which the school system produces and on the consequent appraisals of the kind of knowledge which is appropriate for educational purposes. In most cases, the focus has been on the learner. Child-centrism has resulted in the recognition of the early age at which cultural attitudes begin to be formed and to affect educational achievement. It also has highlighted the importance of various forms of linguistic interaction between child and care-taker, such as that to which Daphne Brown, in her From Mother Tongue to English (1979) attempts to apply Piaget's term 'egocentric speech'. At the later stages of schooling, child-centrism, by demonstrating the need for learning activities to be seen to be purposeful, has pointed the way to syllabus negotiation, and to the development of interactive techniques of discovery which validate the skills already possessed by pupils within a particular class, and which then extends those skills and interests in ways which encourage socialisation and co-operation at the same time. The logical extension of such learner-centre pedagogy into language teaching demands that greater account be taken of the languages which are spoken by signficiant sections of the school-aged population.

Such account would clearly complement the concern of educators in general, and of language teachers in particular, to organise a framework of learning activities which can encourage the potential contribution to be made by diverse cultural groups in our society. As well as benefitting minority pupils, the framework needs to extend the benefits of living in a pluralist society to all. It can do this by increasing the self-confidence of the individual child, and by eliminating the kinds of ignorance which lead to blind prejudice. The DES (1971) expressed these purposes very clearly in its survey of The educational needs of immigrants as fully involving all pupils and students in the life of the school or college while at the same time permitting the expression of differences of attitudes, beliefs and customs, language and culture that are not only held in esteem by those who profess them but which may eventually enrich the main stream of our cultural and social tradition.

Diversification in foreign language provision and teacher shortage

So long have the languages of minority communities been neglected as a resource that the DES itself admits that skills and opportunities of universal value might, in fact, be withering away. Almost a whole generation after workers from the poorer parts of Europe and the Commonwealth began settling in the United Kingdom, the same questions are being asked: 'far more pupils than in the past now have a first language which is not English or Welsh. This constitutes a valuable resource, for them and for the nation. How should mother-tongue teaching for such pupils be accommodated within modern language provision so that this resource does not wither away and the pupils may retain contact with their own communities?' (DES, 1981).

The very way this question is formulated implies that mother-tongue maintenance has to be integrated with provision for those monolingual pupils for whom additional linguistic, and consequently cognitive exposure, is seen as a legitimate goal.

Within the sets of objectives which are generally advanced for modern languages in the school curriculum there seems to be no reason, other than the supply of teachers, which can justify offering the same language to every pupil. George Varnava, formerly Head of Modern Languages at Holland Park School, has pointed out the advantages of allowing pupils to differentiate between different languages in the same way as they can between different sciences when choosing options, 'because often there is no other subject in the curriculum that is even remotely comparable with French.' In his book (Varnava, 1975) he goes on to assert: 'If it is insisted that every pupil should learn a foreign language, it should also be ensured that the experience gained is as rich as possible and that as much as possible is learnt in the time devoted to it. If a pupil undertakes a three year course, his achievement may be greater, for example, in Spanish or German than in French'. It may, of course be even greater in one of the languages used by a confident minority in a school's population.

Attempts to counteract the shortage of available teachers in less commonly taught languages such as Russian and Spanish, to say nothing of Arabic and Chinese, have met with minimal success despite a growing lobby reiterating the view that diversification in foreign language teaching is generally desirable. The National Association of Language Advisers in a statement concerned primarily with languages in the 16-19 curriculum in comprehensive schools have argued: 'The notion that adequate diversification of foreign language teaching can be achieved through second or third foreign language courses (leaving French as the undisputed first foreign language) has proved illusory. No major shift in the balance or range of languages as outlined above would be possible unless languages other than French were progressively introduced as first foreign language in schools, or perhaps more realistically, as joint alternative first foreign language with French where school size permits'. (NALA, 1981). Here then is a practical argument to support the moral, social and psychological points of view in favour of parity for community languages with French and German in the main stream timetable.

Strategy for interactive teaching and teacher training for community languages

More effort seems to have been expended to date in the formidable task of equipping native speakers of English with sufficient knowledge and communicative competence to allow them to teach the traditional target languages such as French, than has been applied to equipping people who are already bilingual with the methodologies and materials for teaching the languages which they already know well. Once trained, such a corps of teachers would have to be deployed where their influence could be most immediately productive.

Towards this end, efforts in the different sectors, from universities and teacher training institutes down to primary schools and nurseries, would need to be coordinated into a mutually beneficial process.

It is less appropriate to speak of language teaching in the initial years than it is to refer to the processes of language acquisition: social interaction and concept formation need to be developed simultaneously with linguistic development in the formative years. Under optimum conditions the bilingual child's languages would be developed in parallel by the environment of the nursery or reception class. Given that at this stage it may well be counterproductive to seek to communicate widely in languages in which nursery nurses themselves are not fully fluent, the task of training suitable staff from the language communities themselves remains an urgent priority for the tertiary sector of education.

The use of each child's mother tongue need not necessarily be total, as long as crucial developmental processes are not discouraged by monolingual teachers. There is, of course, no reason why a nursery teacher, regardless of his or her own mother tongue, should not be taught certain functions in all the languages of the children present for the purposes of greeting them, consoling them, giving them vital instructions, and so on. Story books printed with captions in various languages and culturally familiar objects in pictures and for use as toys can also assist in reducing the alienation which must affect children who speak a language not shared by anyone else at the nursery. Such valuable improvements as can be immediately introduced by monolingual but sensitive teachers cannot, however, be seen as an adequate substitute for the greater involvement of fully prepared bilingual staff. Laszlo Dezsö's suggestions are an example of how such teachers could be trained (Dezsö, 1979).

In the event of mother-tongue maintenance being generalised across the initial stages of maintained education, then the forms of provision relevant in primary, secondary, further and higher education institutions could be correspondingly improved. If children were entering primary schools confident that the language spoken in their community was fully recognised and used by their new teachers, the changes are that by the age of eleven they would be fully literate in more than one language. To some extent then, they could service the community language classes in which they found themselves by acting as models for constructive interaction with pupils wishing to acquire additional languages.

For the time being, however, we are working in a political context where mother tongues are by and large discouraged or ignored, so that the knock-on effect just posited tends, in fact, to operate in reverse. Because school students will by and large have been deprived of elements of their cultural inheritance by successive negative experiences, what was obviously relevant for the nursery school will tend to remain so for the primary stage. In other words provision for five-year olds upwards may well have to compensate for damage done by earlier neglect, as well as providing a language framework appropriate to normally confident and inquisitive pupils. Again, what is true for primary students in terms of a framework which itself facilitates language learning is unlikely to have been provided, so that the same immediate needs will at least be carried forward even if learning difficulties have not been compounded by psychological barriers.

Until a much fuller initial linguistic training can be offered to much larger numbers of bilingual junior and middle school teachers, prospects in the primary sector of education remain the most bleak, with Head teachers usually lacking the staff to cater for even the most common mother tongues present in their intake. It was incidentally a similar shortage of primary trained language teachers that was blamed for the postponing of French until the secondary school.

Of the positions supporting mother-tongue maintenance, the arguments that instruction in the first years of schooling should begin in the mother tongue, and that bilingualism need not affect overall achievement adversely seem in Britain to be gaining acceptance as far as nursery and reception class provision is concerned.

The degree of success obtained in the extension of community languages to pupils between six and eleven can undoubtedly be enhanced by progress made not only at lower but also at higher levels. If, for example, in nursery, infant and junior schools, sixth formers can be encouraged to provide bilingual support at least at story time, the current erosion of status and skills may be somewhat reduced, and the home-school threshold made less of a hurdle.

Secondary schools with the additional resources that result from sheer size and from the maturity of older pupils are well placed to spearhead the integration of community languages into general educational provision. Head teachers have the freedom to deploy existing staff and resources according to the particular needs of the school's intake. Greater flexibility in the timetabling of options assists the introduction of new subjects from time to time. This freedom to manoeuvre has led to a variety of community language courses from eleven, thirteen or even fourteen to 'O' level and CSE. For sixteen-to-nineteen-year olds provision ranges from traditional 'A' level classes to non-examination classes linked with community service.

The 'A' level candidates and community service volunteers of today may well provide us with the community language teachers of tomorrow.

Tailor-made language policies in schools

Recent surveys of linguistic diversity amongst pupils have pointed to the value for each school in surveying its intake, and to develop a specific language policy geared to the needs and resources of that intake. By and large it has been a piecemeal recognition of needs in individual schools, rather than a concerted national or local policy, which has resulted in those advances which have so far been made towards a generally valid language policy, at least in inner-city schools.

Fortunately, many of these piecemeal gains are being consolidated by the few existing programmes of in-service training in centres which maintain close liaison with a number of their local schools. It is precisely this closeness of links with schools that has meant that those institutions, which have specialised in in-service provision for local teachers, have been able to keep abreast of productive developments in language across the curriculum, in study skills and in linguistic diversity. Such institutions are ideally placed to play a key role in the future training of community language teachers along the lines suggested in the section Attentative scheme of training below.

The presence in inner-city schools of large numbers of students whose first language is not English has been instrumental in focussing attention on the position of language in, and across, the curriculum. Much of this attention, naturally enough, was directed initially towards the teaching of standard English for academic and social purposes. The resultant improvements in terms of teaching materials and methodology have benefitted not only learners of English as a second language, but have been generalised in some respects to all students, most notably to those who normally use a non-standard dialect of English. The consideration given to study skills for underachieving pupils similarly has produced a useful spin-off for entire school populations, in the breaking down of academic assignments into the individual skills required to complete them satisfactorily.

In asking Dr J A van Ek (1976) to revise the Threshold Level for use in school education the Committee for General and Technical Education of the Council of Europe recommended that the redraft should 'include a methodological initiation which would, on the one hand, facilitate continued study of the language, and, on the other hand, make it possible to acquire a sufficient understanding of the learning-processes used, so that these may be profitably applied to the study of other languages'. This plea for the inclusion of acquiring methods of the successful learning of foreign languages as one of the explicit aims of the school service is further supplemented by the positions argued by Godfrey and Hawkins (1979) on the need to combine foreign language study with the study of English, and on the need for a study of language in itself.

Such studies of language and language learning need never become solely academic exercises in any multilingual school; the languages and dialects and codes studied could easily be drawn from those actually in use in and around the school. Bilingual children are themselves well placed to exemplify some of the processes involved in language differentiation, and the relationships they form can have a catalytic effect in encouraging reciprocal discoveries. In introducing a particular community language as an educational target, curriculum planners need to bear in mind John Wright's proviso that the motive for introducing minority languages into the learning situation must be 'utilitarian', not 'tokenist'. He points out:

attempts to use languages in a non-utilitarian way, i.e. displaying different scripts on notice boards, having posters headed: 'This is the way we say hello in all of our different languages' are of real but limited use. The danger is that they can too easily appear as a form of tokenism - to minority language children, who, once they realise that they are not actually required to use their own languages will quickly lose interest in its being displayed. And the majority language group will, after the initial novelty, simply assume that other people's languages are there for trivial purposes and not real and valuable tools.' (Wright, 1980) This argument will be further developed by the application of needs analysis to the language environment of multilingual schools. Without first determining the possible uses of a particular language, teachers will find it impossible to devise a course of language instruction which can generate pupil motivation.

In the primary sector, teachers involved in the Brandford MOTET Project listed more than twenty potential uses for an Asian language, a proportion of which included extending cognitive exposure for monolingual English-speaking pupils (MOTET, 1981).

Just as in the conducting of mixed-ability English classes it has been shown to be valuable to structure the teaching in such a way as to stimulate mutually beneficial interaction between pupils at different levels of maturity and linguistic competence, so through the deliberate teaching of community languages will it prove possible within a clearly utilitarian context to achieve many, if not all, of the broad educational aims traditionally claimed for the teaching of foreign (and classical) languages.

Broad aims for language teaching in a multilingual context

Community languages can undoubtedly occupy a useful position within a general strategy for a linguistic education in which teachers of first, second and additional languages can coordinate their efforts at all levels towards helping students undergoing compulsory schooling to:

(1)   use language(s) and the relevent media appropriately for academic, occupational and social purposes;

(2)   develop intellectual skills of general application, including analysis, categorisation, comparing and contrasting, criticism, defining, drawing of inferences, logical reasoning, memorisation, scanning, skimming, summarising, synthesis;

(3)   gain some understanding of the processes used in acquiring a language, and to apply these to the study of such further languages as may be appropriate;

(4)   acquire knowledge of the modest collection of technical terms useful in the discussion of language;

(5)   become aware of the diversity of language and to realise that in linguistic terms no one system of language is inferior to any other;

(6)   reflect personal experience and a confident sense of personal identity, self-esteem and worth;

(7)   widen their experience of other cultures within the local community and beyond it, and to empathise with members of minority groups;

(8)   become aware of how language and the media can be deployed against objectivity, to produce stereotyping, racism and sexism;

(9)   respond sensitively to a wide variety of art forms, in addition to those which are dependent on the use of language, viz literature and film;

(10)   appreciate human achievements, aspirations and criteria of aesthetic value.

The above list was drawn initially from a number of official documents (most notably from the HM Inspectorate Working Paper of December 1977 on Curriculum 11-16) for use by teachers involved in the Alperton High School Mother Tongue Project. The list subsequently underwent some revisions for inclusion in the papers of the Schools Council conference, September 1981, on 'Examining in a multicultural society'.

THE IMMEDIATE NEEDS OF COMMUNITY LANGUAGE TEACHERS

Many of the innovations of the last decade have been shown to point in the same general direction in corroborating the potential contribution of community languages to the improvement of comprehensive education. Implementation of such perspectives however demands a teaching force with a much greater knowledge of language and languages than is currently available in schools. Of the teachers in British schools who have skills in languages other than English the vast majority are employed to teach only French: their performance is rated very low by HM Inspectorate, both in terms of observed practice and in terms of the results obtained which are marked by a very high dropout rate. The deciding factor as to whether additional languages can be offered seems always to be reducible, moreover, to the problem of staffing. The vicious circle of shortage of available staff, which leads to a shortage of suitable materials and which dissuades schools, then colleges, then universities from recognising or offering less commonly taught languages can only be broken at the level of teacher training.

This is equally true for the minority languages spoken in the British Isles. There can be, by definition, no shortage of people with a native competence in their respective community languages. But even if those native speakers happen to be graduates in their own languages, as some are, even if they happen to be trained teachers, as some are, there still exists an enormous gap to be filled in their development of appropriate teaching methodologies to enable them to help to exploit the richness of linguistic diversity only recently fully recognised in inner city schools.

In terms of personal qualitites it would naturally be expected that teachers accepted for training would share a belief that cultural diversity is a valid goal in itself, and that consequently the culture that each child brings to school is worth preserving and enhancing. Bilingual projects elsewhere have stressed this need to respect the child and the culture he or she brings to school, by way of a commitment to enrich the child's positive self-image.

Candidates for any immediate scheme of training would need to be able to demonstrate their competence, both written and spoken, in their community language as well as in English. Some types of self-scoring answer sheet, or self-assessment forms as have been proposed for the Council of Europe by M Oskarsson may well be useful here.

In the initial stages of evolving satisfactory teacher strategies it would be useful to give priority to teachers who already have some experience of language teaching, either in mainstream or voluntary schools. Encouragement also needs to be given to qualified teachers who are bilingual but who are currently working as general subject teachers in primary schools, or even in other disciplines in secondaries. Their expertise would be particularly useful because of the educational content they could add to the teaching of language. The growing acceptance since the Bullock Report of the notion that every teacher is in any case a teacher of language carries with it the implication that very few teachers in our schools have been adequately prepared for the linguistic roles which they inevitably play. It would seem therefore relevant to suggest that the course outlined in the section on training below should eventually become part of every teacher's initial training.

Knowledge of community attitudes

The future of community languages in the UK in the short term depends very heavily on those members of linguistic minorities who are already involved in some way in the educational process. They may be qualified teachers who are involved at various levels and in various subjects; they may be language teachers, involved either in English as a second language or in whatever provision has been won for their mother tongue in the maintained or the voluntary sector. Even if they hold a degree in their mother tongue, they are unlikely to have been adequately prepared for the tasks involved in the introduction of their language into the mainstream curriculum.

A Tosi has detailed in his supporting paper the complexity of issues surrounding mother-tongue teaching in the context of second language learning, issues which make this context unique.

There are a number of foci to which the teacher of community languages will have to give attention besides the individual learner and, of course, the language itself. In addition to the intrinsic difficulties of the standard forms of language to be taught, the teacher will need to have knowledge of the social implications attached to its variants. Even for most standardised languages with the possible exception of English, French and German, there is a dearth of published teaching materials. Such shortages are exacerbated by the presence of several distinct and equally valid dialects of the community languages so far identified. Tosi has dealt at length with this particular focus: it should be sufficient here to emphasize the sort of information which classroom practitioners will need to be sure of before even undertaking to teach their language.

It involves above all a focus on the community, and on the culture of that community, as viewed internally. A thorough knowledge of attitudes, such as can only be adequately determined by proper survey techniques, will determine the viability of teaching a particular language a particular way within the context of a particular school in a particular catchment area. Additional information about the social, religious, and economic aspirations of a linguistic community should play a role in determining the content of the language to be taught in terms of the background topics dealt with in the teaching. Local attitudes will thus influence profoundly the place of the community language within the general curriculum, and the weighting put behind the objectives sought through its introduction. One implication is that where a community has failed to maintain the status of the language for its own members, it may well prove to be counterproductive to attempt to teach it in the local school.

To increase their chances of success, community language teachers, therefore, need to be able to determine the attitude of the local community to the various languages that it might be proposed to offer on the three clines suggested in Fig. 1. They need also some knowledge of the theories concerning multilingual/multicultural education and of the rights of linguistic minorities under existing social and educational legislation. Willingness and ability to co-operate with the local community may extend as far as involvement in campaigning for the above rights. For more minutely itemised lists of the attitudes and skills to be sought in teachers for bilingual/bicultural situations, some American manuals such as Casso (1976) offer a useful starting point.

Analysis and management of different levels of competence

If within an actively multilingual policy, the languages of minority communities are to be fostered as they should be by schools, then they must be fostered in classes which for social reasons cannot consist exclusively of mother-tongue speakers.

John Wright (1980) is very clear about this. Two of the criteria he lists in Bilingualism and schooling in multilingual Britain clarify the point. He insists: 'Provide language learning opportunities, and the opportunity of becoming bilingual, to all students – even though a very small minority of English-speaking students would take up the option'; and further, 'Never segregate the minority group for mother tongue learning ... without explicitly inviting all pupils/students to join the group'. In the initial lessons there is likely to be a whole range of differential proficiency along the continuum between native speakers and complete beginners. To cope with such hetero-geneity a teacher will need a stock of learning activities designed for pairs and groups, as well as individually programmed exercises operating at various levels around a common theme. Under such circumstances it is equally essential to devise ways of monitoring closely what each learner has succeeded so far in achieving.

Eric Hawkins (1981), in analysing the differences between typical classroom situations for learning a first and a foreign language, pointed out that the ratio of model users of the target language to beginners went very much in the favour of first language classes.

Community language classes, unless, contrary to advice, they are restricted to first language users only, will come somewhere between Hawkins' polar opposite first and foreign contexts. When community languages are taught in schools where a high proportion of the population uses them, the presence of native speakers will considerably enhance the learning environment.

Because even those pupils who identify with a linguistic community will have had varying degrees of exposure to the language, teachers will need conceptual tools to determine the range of starting points at the outset of a course of instruction. In secondary schools, Fig. 2, a form adapted from Oskarsson's Approaches to self assessment in foreign language learning, may well prove useful.

FIGURE 1

CHART OF ATTITUDES REGARDING USE OF THE COMMUNITY LANGUAGE
adapted from Krear (1969)

	At Home	In the Community	At School
N	–Hostility to culture of origin		
E			
G	–Discouraged in favour of majority language of country of residence	–Repressed, for purposes of total integration	–Prohibited
A			
T			
I			
V	–Non-standard variant discouraged in favour of national standard from country of origin	–Language of local ascendancy preferred	–Ridiculed
E			

			–Ignored
N	–Used by one parent only	–Used for religion	–Permitted
E			
U			–Used by teachers
T			
R			
A	–Used by parents but not by children	–Used in shops, and for other social, economic purposes	–Taught out of school hours
L			
			–Native users entered for exams

			–Books in library
P			–Minor component in some subjects
O	–Encouraged by constant use in the home	–Taught in community schools	
S			
I			–Target language in open option system
T			
I			
V	–Literacy taught explicitly at home	–Cultivated by cinema, theatre, etc	–Medium of instruction
E			

FIGURE 2

SELF ASSESSMENT FORM FOR LANGUAGE STUDENTS IN SECONDARY SCHOOLS

Read through all the statements below with the help of your teacher. Then place ticks in all the boxes beside statements which apply to you.

.1   LISTENING

☐ 0 I have only just begun to understand anything at all in the language.

☐ 1 I understand common words and phrases if they are spoken slowly and clearly.

☐ 2 I can follow and understand the main points about everyday things, but often need to have things repeated, or made clearer.

☐ 3 I can follow and understand the main points of a conversation when people are speaking clearly.

☐ 4 I understand practically everything that is said in the language when people are speaking normally.

.2   SPEAKING

☐ 0 I have only just begun to be able to say anything at all in the language.

☐ 1 I can say some words and simple phrases.

☐ 2 I can ask and answer simple questions about the time, food, prices, and directions.

☐ 3 I can make myself understood in most everyday situations, but I cannot always find the words for what I want to say.

☐ 4 I speak the language fluently: because I have a large vocabulary I seldom have to search for words.

.3   READING

☐ 0 I have only just begun to learn to read anything in the language at all.

☐ 1 I understand the meaning of simple written instructions about finding the way, the time, the date, etc.

(Figure 2 continued)

☐ 2 I understand the essential things in simple texts dealing with familiar subjects such as food, clothes, leisure interests, etc.

☐ 3 I like to read simple books and understand most of what I read. I would for example understand most of a normal private letter.

☐ 4 I understand everything, or almost everything written in the language, although there may be words I would need to look up in the dictionary.

.4 WRITING

☐ 0 I have only just begun to learn to write the language.

☐ 1 I know the alphabet and can write down some simple words.

☐ 2 I can write very simply about myself.

☐ 3 I could write a letter that someone else could understand, but it might have some mistakes.

☐ 4 I write the language easily and usually correctly.

(Adapted from Oskarsson: Approaches to self assessment in foreign language learning. Pergamon, 1979.)

Individualised instruction

Clearly, the tasks of a community language teacher extend beyond those of a traditional language teacher, who may be equipped with a particular set syllabus and with appropriate course books, so that he or she can concentrate all efforts on performance in the classroom. It has already been pointed out that the teacher of French or German is frequently the only nexus between the subject and the students, with the resultant reinforcement of traditional pedagogy – the teacher with the jug of knowledge filling empty vessels.

Such a narrow pedagogy is bound to fail where students are clearly bringing their own very different language skills and strategies to contribute in their learning of forms of language which are already used by some of their classmates. Teachers of French and German often assume that all of their student are starting out from the same point at the begining of the course: because this is patently not the case for community language teachers they will have to focus on each learner in very precise ways. It will be necessary to discover language(s) spoken in the student's home, the associated cultural and other assumptions with regard to school work, the particular learning strategies favoured by the student. The initial focus on each learner will have to take into account each of the variables which Tosi has listed in his paper 'Materials for mother-tongue teaching in the context of second-language learning'. For example, any attempt to diagnose particular learning difficulties will demand relevant knowledge of language acquisition processes, cognitive developmental processes, as well as psychology, and sociometrics within and beyond the classroom. All these factors will be seen to be relevant to the motivation of individual pupils as are the recognisable points of difference between the target language and the pupil's mother tongue. The status of the targe language within the surrounding society and its identifiable use value for both long and short term goals are bound to influence progress just as significantly as the relative degree of exposure to English and the target language.

American experts in the field of foreign language teaching, most notably Renée Disick, and Howard Altman, have studied in some detail the range of successful learning styles which may be present in one classroom. Disick (1975) deals constructively with management problems, such as materials storage and record keeping; she also provides sample lesson plans and learning packet instructions which are sufficiently flexible to allow adaptation for varying teaching contexts. Altman and James (1981) in Foreign language teaching: meeting individual needslist no less than fourteen dimensions of individual difference in second language learning. A questionnaire, like the one designed for use some time during the first year of a course in Gujarati (or Urdu) at Alperton High School helps a teacher to take account of some of the dimensions encountered whilst working with community languages. This questionnaire (Fig. 3) additionally helps in the negotiation of a relevant syllabus for a particular class with its list of topics for prioritisation.

FIGURE 3

COMMUNITY LANGUAGE LEARNERS' QUESTIONNAIRE

Name ....

What schools have you attended besides this one? ....

What language(s) do you use at home? ....

Which other language can you use at all? ....

What made you decide to learn Gujarati/Urdu?

☐   I want to find out more about the people who use it.

99

(Figure 3 continued)

☐ I want to find out more about the countries where it is used.

☐ I am already good at it.

☐ I can speak it but I want to learn to read and write it.

☐ It's easier than French for me.

☐ I want to know how to go about learning several languages.

Any other reasons ....

What opportunities do you get to speak Gujarati/Urdu outside the classroom? ....
....

How do you intend to use Gujarati/Urdu after the course?

☐ as an exam-qualification for a job

☐ to speak friends and join activities with them

☐ when I am travelling

Any other reasons ....

What do you enjoy most about the lessons? ....

What do you enjoy least about the lessons? ....

What else would you like to do in the lessons? ....

I would like to learn more Gujarati/Urdu to help me understand, talk and write about these topics

☐ School   ☐ Food, drink and cookery

☐ Family   ☐ Sports and games

☐ House and Home   ☐ Transport

☐ Clothes and fashion   ☐ Money

☐ Festivals   ☐ Shopping

☐ Geography   ☐ History

☐ Hotels, Restaurants, Cafes   ☐ Music and songs

Design for suitable courses

Native speakers of the languages of minority communities would not face the same problems as, for example, teachers of French who may not have the necessary proficiency in the target language to teach it commumicatively. But they are likely to share – with linguists – the difficulty of describing how that language functions. The subject they are presenting has, like any other, to be analysed and broken down in such a way as to present it in an easily assimilable form.

In all school provision for community languages the language taught will have to be capable of being put directly into use. Purposeful learning syllabuses will arise either from an analysis of needs, or from a more structured pre-existent threshold-type enumeration of those basic words, constructions, notions and functions which are intuitively believed to be of general use, but which can be submitted for negotiation with students. In whichever way such syllabuses are arrived at, they are likely to be quite different from the grammatical/lexical teaching lists already used for many foreign languages and for some community languages.

It is probably accurate to say that the approaches to a more practical approach began with word frequency studies and other systematic attempts to reduce the amount of essential vocabulary entailed in the learning of a new language. A number of basic vocabularies in various languages including Urdu are now based on frequency studies. Perhaps the most celebrated of these is <u>Le francais fondamental</u> produced by a team at the Centre de Recherche Pedagogique under Professor Gougenheim; their basic 'première série' contained 1400 words.

The application of such ideas to a Unit/Credit system of modern language learning for adults initially has led to the formulation of a standardised initial syllabus containing, alongside an inventory of some 1050 words the basic functions and notions of a target language as it may be used in a certain limited number of commonly met situations. The specification by van Ek (1976) of a Threshold Level for language learning has been turned into a viable survival syllabus by L G Alexander who has listed the necessary exponents for English. Similar lists of exponents are being compiled for many other languages, of which perhaps the most significant from the point of view of developing UK community languages are the projects for Spanish, Italian and Greek.

A complementary development has been the formulation of graded objectives for foreign languages in schools: graded tests which have been devised for Oxfordshire, Yorkshire and elsewhere, underpinned as they are by more satisfactory definitions of linguistic competence, have resulted in great improvements in terms of increased motivation in school programmes. The wider application of these techniques to the languages which are already present in the school environment should enhance this trend.

The distillation of a language down to the minimum components required for survival in predefined situations will undoubtedly serve the purposes of those students who are starting from fresh to learn a community language, and of students who, in spite of having some relatives who speak the language, have little experience of using it themselves.

Even students who may be quite fluent in speaking the language may still require tuition in order to be able to read and write it. For such students there should perhaps be more emphasis on analysis of the language in question, in terms of its phonology, the derivation of its vocabulary, its structures and the rules according to which the language functions. Such knowledge could be related to a study of English, and could follow quite closely the stages by which beginners can learn, so the models in a mixed competence classroom could contribute to the progress of the others, and vice versa. A two-tier course of this nature would conform well to the broad aims specified above on p 91. Wherever possible aims should be made explicit to pupils.

The earliest reading materials could, without being insulting, still be based largely on the functions of language relevant to complete beginners in the situations they are quite likely to encounter. Although such a postion should not be allowed to obliviate fantasy or the exotic, the initial contexts have to be in the urban British environment familiar to most of the students. Those who use the target language in the home are almost certain to make much more rapid progress in reading than complete beginners: the discrepancy need not be disastrous as long as the skilled readers progress to matter which genuinely interests them, as well as being given the range to begin writing primers, and recording dialogues for the less skilled.

The informational content of intermediate and advanced stages of a course has to continue to excite the students' interest and to promote their willingness to communicate. Such interests can be determined by negotiation with the students: an adequate way of doing this is to tabulate a series of possibilities for them to prioritise. Members of the local communities could be invited to give demonstrations in practical subjects like cookery or crafts, or even to teach more academic subjects like geography or history through the medium of the target language.

For some time to come the available exams will continue to exercise a powerful influence on the design of courses. Composition and translation (which can in the case of community languages become quite a practical skill as can interpreting) are still essential skills for those due to be examined at '0' level; 'A' level additionally involves literary studies. The available exams, like the available materials, and indeed the available methodologies form three of the major constraints which school syllabus design will have to take account of.

Materials: a checklist of criteria

Materials which have been imported from the country of origin for use in the teaching of the languages of minority communities may not always match the standards of presentation and the methodologies to which students in Britain are accustomed. More disturbingly, unless they are purpose-made the materials may base themselves upon experiences which are totally unusual for inner city children in the UK. The set of questions below was evolved at Alperton High School for evaluating the materials sent to the Community Language Project by the Brent Community Librarian.

.1   Utility   +   -

.1.1   Are the aims specified explicitly?   ☐
.1.2   Are the methodological procedures made clear for the
        teacher?   ☐
.1.3   Are the materials motivating and enjoyable to use?   ☐
.1.4   Are the instructions unambiguous for the students?   ☐
.1.5   Do they allow for creativity as well as for repetition?   ☐
.1.6   Can they be used easily in a variety of ways,
.1.7   i.e. with individual students?   ☐
.1.8   with a whole class?   ☐
.1.9   in pairs?   ☐
.1.10   in groups?   ☐
.1.11   Do they coordinate a wide range of skills,
.1.12   i.e. listening?   ☐
.1.13   reading?   ☐
.1.14   speaking?   ☐
.1.15   writing?   ☐
.1.16   Can we say that there is no skill consistently
        neglected?   ☐
.1.17   Are model answers available to facilitate feedback
        on errors?   ☐
.1.18   Are the materials cheap to buy/reproduce?   ☐
.1.19   Do they succeed in their aims?   ☐

.2   Appropriacy

.2.1   Is the language at the right level of simplicity?   ☐
.2.2   Does the language fit the needs of the students?   ☐
.2.3   Is the language presented in an authentic context?   ☐
.2.4   Does the use of language correspond to that of native
        users?   ☐
.2.5   Is the language practised in meaningful ways?   ☐
.2.6   Are the underlying concepts adequately explained?   ☐
.2.7   Is the informational content relevant?   ☐
.2.8   Does the content reflect a sensitivity towards the
        way in which the specific culture is viewed internally?   ☐

.3   Layout and Presentation

.3.1   Do the materials look interesting?
.3.2   Are they well organised and clear?
.3.3   Do they avoid racial stereotyping?
.3.4   Do they avoid sexual stereotyping?
.3.5   Is there any visual presentation,
.3.6   i.e. in the form of pictures?
.3.7   maps?
.3.8   charts?
.3.9   Are the illustrations pleasant to look at?
.3.10   Are they juxtaposed with the language they
         contextualise?
.3.11   Are the illustrations culturally diverse?

                    Total number of positive points
                    Total number of negative points

Appropriate methodologies

There can be no question here of specifying a particular methodology
for community languages: to do so would be unjustifiable, even ir-
responsible. Of the syllabus types available to suit utilitarian
purposes, however, it would seem that a topic-centred one may well
be the best, allowing a flexible balance between controlled work
with a whole class, and group work or individualisation in order to
cater for different learning levels and styles. This recommendation
itself has certain far-reaching methodological implications.

With regard to initial literacy alone, it does appear to be an
impossible task to provide in a single framework of teacher training
for such a wide range of languages as is at present in use amongst
communities in the UK. The range involves alphabetical systems which
differ in varying degrees from the Roman one - Cyrillic, Devanagri,
Arabic, Greek and so on, to say nothing of the ideographic forms of
writing used for Chinese languages.

Nevertheless, current moves inspired by a psycholinguistic approach
to reading have tended to favour the whole word or even whole
sentence methods.   Certainly there is a wide range of available
techniques, some of which - speech-based strategies, matching games,
reading laboratories, etc - are likely to be of general use.

There is a natural tendency for language teachers to fall back on
the methods of teaching through which they themselves learned successfully. It does seem, moreover, to be true that as long as a teacher is convinced by the effectiveness of a particular methodology,
then he or she can achieve satisfactory results by using it. Under
these circumstances it would be foolhardy to abandon well-tried

strategies in favour of much-acclaimed but unproved panaceas. When particular methods, be they old or new, are tried out in the wrong context, or in otherwise unfavourable circumstances, and are shown to produce unsatisfactory results, then other approaches have to be sought. Methodologies must be evaluated according to a simple, practical criterion: do they work?

The ability to assess one's own needs as a teacher is every bit as important as the ability to assess a student's or a community's needs. Not all of the problems met by community language teachers are going to be specific to that discipline: some help can be sought from colleagues working in related fields. Indeed, a number of the documents presented in previous years to the National Congress on Languages in Education encourage the view that specialists in their respective fields of English as a second language, English as a foreign language, English mother-tongue and foreign language teaching can learn much from each other, and that, therefore, the training of teachers in these fields should occur within a properly integrated framework. Teachers of mother tongues other than English, although at present very much the poor relations in comparison with teachers in the latter three fields, can also play a vital role in overcoming fragmentation in the theory and practice of language teaching in this country, especially when the languages used by minority communities become more generally recognised as a genuine pedagogic resource.

Up until the impetus provided by the EEC Commission, very little encouragement had been given to any kind of provision other than voluntary for developing the linguistic resources already present in our multiracial society. By far the largest amounts of investment in language teaching in this country have been previously directed towards teaching English as a foreign language, with French, German, and a few other European languages receiving occasional support. From the audio-visual methods of presentation pioneered in the fifties, to the structural/situational approaches and Caleb Gattegno's 'Silent Way' of the sixties, to the notional/functional or communicative syllabuses of the seventies, each set of innovations has started out from research into those languages which have international status, most notably English. The keynote of the programme here described is the transfer wherever possible and productive of those analytical theories and pedagogic techniques to languages which have so far received little attention, or investment.

A major task then, here, is to decide which of the advanced methodologies of foreign language teaching can be applied to UK minority languages, and which strategies can be borrowed from innovations in primary and secondary school techniques in English (as a mother tongue) and English as a second language.

Insofar as they relate to specific languages, some of the areas of enquiry suggested in the following section are still very much in pioneering stages, as is indeed the whole field of multilingualism in the UK. Nevertheless, many units proposed are already offered in a number of institutions and require only that change of emphasis which teachers from minority communities are likely to produce for themselves.

An in-service tutor group of Panjabi teachers from the London Borough of Ealing, which began meeting in November 1981 under the direction of Sat Gupta, Advisory Teacher for South Asian Languages, prioritised their subsequent informational needs in the following order:

(1) Methods for teaching initial literacy, with reading taking precedence over writing;

(2) Methods for encouraging listening and speaking, including a relevant knowledge of phonetics;

(3) Techniques for teaching and marking translation;

(4) Strategies for classroom management, especially involving individualisation, group work and role play.

Two prerequisites which this particular group of teachers rated much lower but which would have to precede any short practical course are:

(5) Ways of assessing the variables affecting each child's progress in learning;

(6) Components of syllabus design.

The high priority attached to translation is likely to be a washback effect of the existing examination system: other community language teachers have rated much more highly interactive strategies for encouraging oracy and have suggested the inclusion of techniques for teaching interpreting and literary studies, both of which would be for use with the sixteen to nineteen age range and beyond.

A TENTATIVE SCHEME OF TRAINING

Spicer, Mittins and Dawson (1978) make a number of points of general relevance which apply directly to the training of teachers of community languages:

'Many of the methodological problems confronting the foreign language teacher also confront the teacher of English as the mother tongue (and indeed confront the teaching profession as a whole), e.g. problems of individualisation of teaching, of mixed ability classes, of the specification and differentiation of objectives, of teacher- learner interaction, of the identification, explanation and treatment of learners' errors, of motivation, of relating what is taught in a particular class to the rest of the curriculum and to the 'real world' outside the school, etc, etc.'

Ways of solving the above methodological problems should form the core of any language teacher's training. The presence in a mainstream English lesson of pupils for whom English is a second language is in some ways comparable to the presence in a foreign language classroom of one or more native speakers of say French or German. Neither situation is new, and both call for such organisational solutions as can allow a teacher to intervene in ways which facilitate an exchange of knowledge and skill between the linguistically competent and those less so. The teaching of community languages in formally unsegregated classes calls for similar solutions.

The choice of components listed in the course outline which follows is based on the assumption that teachers following the courses will be sufficiently fluent in both English and at least one minority community language to be able to decide for themselves which of the methods and ideas presented to them can be most usefully applied to their own teaching.

To judge by the low proportions mentioned in the Bullock Report of trained English specialists in our schools it would seem to be a commonly-held belief that a native competence in a language is sufficient qualification to teach it. And yet equally commonly held must be the truism that a person unaware of the problems posed by the acquisition of their particular skill makes a very poor instructor.

Besides being able to demonstrate their knowledge of the principles of language learning and teaching, especially with regard to the varieties of classroom management suitable to their purposes, candidates would be expected towards the end of their course to display their practical teaching competence. Given the present level of community language studies, they would need to be able to design a satisfactory syllabus for their students as well as a collection of appropriate teaching materials.

Presumably a degree in the target language in this discipline as elsewhere would be the essential qualification for teaching 'A' level students and above. To the basic outline below for advanced classes it would be useful to add components on literary studies, as well as on techniques of interpreting and translation. Bearing in mind the continuing reliance on translation of public exams especially in South Asian languages, it seems such techniques might also be useful for teachers of younger pupils.

A minimum of 150 contact hours would be required to put across the basic content of the course proposed. This does not include reading, observing others teaching or other useful visits. After an extended period of preliminary reading it is assumed that practising teachers would be withdrawn from their duties for one term. Morning seminars over a period of some ten weeks could consolidate their knowledge of the theoretical background required: at least half of each morning would also be given over to workshops to demonstrate practical applications in terms of teaching materials. Afternoons would be kept free for visits, classroom observation and eventually microteaching.

In view of the enormous range of languages currently in use in the UK it seems advisable that the basic components should be applicable to virtually any language; account will have to be taken in very general terms of phonologies, grammars and writing systems which do not, for example, use the Roman alphabet.

It is in the nature of such proposals for in-service training in a hitherto relatively untried discipline that they appear rather unstructured. Through the openings that such ventures should create, however, we may move towards that coherent theory of second language learning which previous contributors to NCLE discussions have preferred to the 'heterogeneous assortment of ideas we have today'. Indeed the 'space between' specialist teachers of modern foreign languages and of English as the mother tongue may well be narrowed by teachers of the languages of minority communities. Studies relevant to the latter can be divided into three seemingly neat compartments: 'multilingual/multicultural' education, 'language description and language learning', and 'classroom management, methods and materials'. Each element, which is in fact far from being hermetic, is provided with a list of aims and contents.

The block-by-block elucidation of aims and content includes two essential components for assessing the performance of a teacher who has followed the whole scheme of training. One involves the assessment of the candidate's ability to teach successfully, checking the appropriateness of the activities chosen, as well as their preparation and execution, and the ongoing support provided within the classroom. The other takes the form of three assignments which demonstrate the candidate's ability to prepare effective teaching materials. Given the current state of the teaching of the languages of minority communities, it might be appropriate to expect an extended essay dealing with some particular aspect of the target language and even the outline of a whole syllabus for use by one of the candidate's classes.

Multilingual/multicultural education

(1) Aims:
- to analyse the processes involved in cultural impacting;

- to impart knowledge of the pattern of migration to the UK and the reasons for it as well as the consequent psychological differences which will affect educational provision;

- to investigate the factors producing low and high status in languages and dialects, and their repercussions in schools;

- to review the patterns of provision for bilingual education in Sweden, the USA and Canada, the Soviet Union and the EC.

- to investigate the proper place for the languages of minority communities within the overall curriculum of UK schools;

- to assess the extent to which the languages of such communities can relevantly be used as a medium for teaching other skills and informational content;

    to draw practical conclusions for language teachers from the available theories of multicultural education and of cultural transmission

(2) Content:
- patterns of uneven economic development
- patterns of migration
- language evolution and language loyalty
- comparative education with regard to bilingualism
- sociology of education and sociolinguistics
- psychological and psycholinguistic considerations
- bilingualism and biliteracy

Language description and language learning

(1) Aims:
- to analyse the constraints which determine a course of instruction;

- to compare different syllabus types with a view to producing relevant objectives in a target language;

- to present the basic principles useful in describing a specified target language in its oral and written forms;

- to demonstrate the inadequacy of purely grammatical description, and the relevance to language teaching of ideas drawn from the fields of sociolinguistics, discourse analysis, phonology, etc;

- to contrast the systems identified in English with those of the target language, given that English is likely to be the one language shared by all participants on the course, as well as being the subject of much innovatory investigation by applied linguists;

- to assess the usefulness of strategies for first languge acquisition to institutionalised language teaching;

- to present criteria for the assessment of students' progress.

.2 Content:
- articulatory phonetics and phonetic transcription
- rhythm, stress and intonation patterns
- received pronunciation and regional accent
- dialectal variation: prescriptive and descriptive approaches
- frequency studies of lexical items
- grammar and syntax
- notions and functions of language
- connected discourse and cohesion
- mother tongue teaching in the context of second language learning
- principles of sequencing and grading
- needs analysis
- error analysis
- explicitness of aims and syllabus negotiation

Classroom management, methods and materials

.1 Aims:
- to explore justifications for divergent forms of provision;

- to evaluate the various approaches to the teaching of literacy both here and in the country of origin of the target language;

- to investigate methods of developing writing skills, from initial scripts to composition;

- to familiarise the trainee teacher with the stock-in-trade procedures of other types of teaching, especially English mother tongue and foreign language teaching, with reference to the design and production of attractive materials. (A set of teaching materials based on topics to be decided by the course organisers will be assessed for the final certificate);

- to indicate possibilities for exploiting language resources existing outside the classroom;

- to assess the place of translation and interpreting in a course of instruction;

- to observe and review methods used for individual, group and whole class teaching in a variety of classes and schools;

- to develop a set of organisational procedures appropriate to the wide range of needs likely to be encountered in classrooms where the languages of minority communities are taught;

- to provide opportunities for trainee teachers to implement the knowledge they have acquired on the course in practice in a local authority or voluntary school. (The practical part of the Certificate should involve an assessment of the candidate's ability to teach at least one model lesson within a collectively agreed syllabus.)

.2 Content:
- keeping adequate records
- programmed learning and self-access materials
- techniques for whole-class teaching
- group work, role play and project work
- games and songs
- the tape recorder and the language laboratory
- using reprographic facilities, visual aids and videotapes
- reading schemes and reading laboratories
- listening exercises and note-taking
- speech-based reading and writing methods
- calligraphy and writing systems
- cloze exercises and other standard procedures
- sentence linking and sequencing
- writing letters, short stories and essays
- correcting written work

* An earlier draft of this paper was prepared for the Working Party on The Languages of Minority Communities during 1981. The author was at the time of writing co-ordination of the Community Language (formerly Mother Tongue) Project in the Alperton High School, Brent.

REFERENCES

ALTMAN, H B and C V James, eds (1981). Foreign language teaching: meeting individual needs. London, New York: Pergamon Press.

BROWN, D (1979). Mother tongue to English: the young child in the multicultural. Cambridge: Cambridge University Press.

CASSO, H (1976). Bilingual/bicultural education and teacher training. Washington, D.C.: National Education Association.

DEPARTMENT OF EDUCATION AND SCIENCE (1981). The education of immigrants. (Education Survey 13.) London: Her Majesty's Stationery Office.

DEPARTMENT OF EDUCATION AND SCIENCE/WELSH OFFICE (1981). The school curriculum. London: Her Majesty's Stationery Office.

DESZO, L (1979). How pre-school teachers could be trained. In: R Freudenstein, ed: Teaching foreign languages to the very young. London, New York: Pergamon Press.

DISICK, R (1975). Individualising language instruction: strategies and methods. New York, Chicago: Harcourt, Brace.

GODFREY, R and E Hawkins (1978). The education of teachers of foreign languages. In: G E Perren, ed: Foreign languages in education. (NCLE Papers & Reports 1.) London: Centre for Information on Language Teaching and Research.

HARDING, A, B Page and S Rowell (1980). Graded objectives in modern languages. London: Centre for Information on Language Teaching and Research, 1980.

HAWKINS, E (1981). Modern languages in the curriculum. Cambridge: Cambridge University Press.

HER MAJESTY'S INSPECTORATE OF SCHOOLS (1978). Curriculum 11-16: working papers by H M Inspectorate: a contribution to current debate. Department of Education and Science.

MOTHER TONGUE AND ENGLISH TEACHING PROJECT (1981). Summary of the report, vols I and II. Bradford: MOTET, pp 17-18.

NATIONAL ASSOCIATION OF LANGUAGE ADVISERS(1981). Foreign languages in schools. NALA.

NATIONAL ASSOCIATION FOR MULTIRACIAL EDUCATION (1981). Mother tongue and minority community languages in education. (Policy statement.) NAME.

NATIONAL CONGRESS ON LANGUAGES IN EDUCATION (1981). Report of Working Party C: A comparison of the various methodologies and materials involved in the teaching of English as a foreign language, modern languages, and the mother tongue, and an examination of their relevance to each other. In: J Davidson, ed: Issues in language education. (NCLE Papers & Reports 3.) London: Centre for Information on Language Teaching and Research.

OSKARSSON, M (1978). Approaches to self-assessment in foreign language learning. Strasbourg, Council of Europe, 1978; Oxford, New York: Pergamon, for and on behalf of the Council of Europe, 1980.

PORCHER, L (1981). The Education of the Children of Migrant Workers in Europe: interculturalism and teacher training, Council of Europe, Strasbourg.

SPICER, A, W Mittins and C Dawson(1978). The education and training of teachers. In: G E Perren (ed): The mother tongue and other languages in education. (NCLE Papers & Reports 2.): London: Centre for Information on Language Teaching and Research

VAN EK, J (1976). The threshold level for modern language learning in schools. First published in mimeograph, 1976. Harlow: Longman, 1977.

VARNAVA, G (1975). Mixed ability teaching in modern languages. Glasgow, London: Blackie.

WRIGHT, J (1980). Bilingualism and schooling in Multilingual Britain. (Occasional Paper 1.) London: Centre for Urban Educational Studies.

PUBLIC EXAMINATIONS IN ETHNIC MINORITY LANGUAGES - AVAILABILITY AND CURRENCY*

Euan Reid
Institute of Education
University of London

AVAILABILITY

This first section of the paper is based on the responses to a circular letter dated January 30 1981 sent to all CSE and GCE examination boards, and to related bodies in the exam field. This circular enquired about which exams were offered by the various boards, whether any special conditions were attached, whether any representations or suggestions had been made about the exams, and whether there were any plans for development in this field. There was a very full response, and the Working Party was therefore able to consider the current situation as laid out in what follows at its June 1981 meeting, and to make a number of recommendations, which are also incorporated in the Working Party's Report.

In July 1981 the draft of this section was then sent for comment back to the exam boards and associated bodies, a number of correction and amendments were made, and the tables on entry statistics added. No updating has been attempted since late 1981, so the position may have changed in some of the Boards by now.

CSE exams

(a) No exams were offered in any mode, no approaches were reported, and no developments were planned by East Anglia, South-East, North, North-West, Yorkshire, Wales, Northern Ireland.

(b) Southern was in a similar position but referred to plans for the assessment of Spanish-English bilingual candidates, arising out of the Board's responsibility for Gibraltar.

(c) East Midlands had recently approved a Mode 3 syllabus in Urdu. A Mode 3 Syllabus in Polish was offered in a single school.

(d) West Yorkshire and Lindsey had a Mode 3 Urdu syllabus in a single school.

(e) London had a Mode 3 Gujarati in operation, and a Mode 3 Urdu at the planning stage.

114

(f) West Midlands had Mode 3 exams in Urdu and Punjabi.

Most of the Boards in their responses stated in some form or other
the 'no demand, therefore no supply' argument, but indicated a
willingness to consider proposals from schools in their areas,
though one mentioned the possible difficulties of finding an
appropriately qualified examiner.

GCE and equivalent exams

(a) Northern Ireland and Welsh Boards, along with Southern Universities and Oxford & Cambridge Joint Board, made no provision,
had received no approaches, and had no plans in this field.
Southern and Welsh Boards indicated that they 'borrow' from
other boards where necessary.

(b) AEB was in a similar position, its presumed involvement in
examining Shona and Afrikaans in South Africa apart, and did
not appear to see a role for itself here; this Board too
mentioned the 'borrowing' facility.

(c) Cambridge Local too seemed to have made provision in connection
with its overseas responsibilities only, from the languages
listed (Afrikaans, Bengali, Hindi, Punjabi and Urdu) apparently
also in Africa. Exams in these languages, known as 'syllabus Y'
are set for candidates taking SC and 'O' level exams in certain
overseas countries other than the mother-tongue country, but
they are available in the UK on request. To date, there
appeared to have been very little take-up here.

(d) The Scottish Board had just introduced Modern Hebrew, and had a
small entry for ordinary grade Portuguese.

This left three Boards making the major provision:-

(1) JMB offered a limited range - Polish, Ukrainian, Punjabi and
Modern Hebrew at 'O' level, and the last two also at 'A' level,
possibly to be joined by Ukrainian. They were all designed and
administered like other modern language exams, seemed to be the
result of specific submission from schools in the JMB region,
and the Board made clear that it would only consider extending
its provision in response to further such demand.

(2) Oxford Local offered 27 languages, Gujarati having been
recently discontinued in favour of borrowing it from London.
The Board's letter indicated that this was partly the result of
recent discussions about rationalisation of provision in the
field in view of small entries. They also indicated that
revision in the form of the exams was unlikely before a new 16+

exam took over 'despite our awareness that in some cases they are unsuitable for the present clientèle: they were based on a traditional French syllabus designed for English learners who had followed a course of tuition in the foreign language, whereas the majority of candidates for most of these subjects in recent years have been native speakers (or children of native speakers) of the languages concerned'. (See the <u>Recent developments</u> section below for change planned by Oxford.)

(3)   London offered up to 25 languages. The regulation stating that, for 'O' levels, 'only one of these subjects may be taken at any one exam' is to be removed with effect from June 1983. The Board's letter also added that 'Those representations which we do receive from time to time concerning the exams in such subjects are usually voicing concern about the difficulty of the papers set, suggesting that an assumption is being made that candidates are bilingual. This is, in fact, comparatively rarely the case and we bear this firmly in mind in setting the papers'. 'The future of exams in these subjects will, of course, be considered in the preparation for the new system of examining at 16+, but syllabus development in this area is at a very early stage.'

The following table is extracted from the more comprehensive one prepared by JMB, dated October 1980, and refers to <u>exams available in 1982</u>. (Brackets indicate those exams which Oxford intended to discontinue after 1982.)

	LONDON 'O'	LONDON 'A'	OXFORD 'O'	OXFORD 'A'	JMB 'O'	JMB 'A'	CAMBRIDGE 'O' SYLLABUS Y
Modern ARABIC			+				
BENGALI	+						+
CHINESE	+	+	+				
Modern GREEK	+	+	+				
GUJARATI	+						
HINDI	+	+	(+)				+
PUNJABI					+	+	+
POLISH	+	+	(+)	(+)	+		
PORTUGUESE	+	+	(+)				
TURKISH	+	+	(+)				
UKRAINIAN					+		
URDU	+	+	(+)				+

116

It is clear from the table that there were exams existing or in prospect at both 'O' and 'A' level in most of the languages of the major linguistic minorities in Britain now, with the notable exception of 'A' levels in Gujarati, Bengali, and Modern Arabic (though there are London and Oxford 'O' and 'A' levels in Classical Arabic). However, the choice that existed in some of the languages at 'O' level (though in none of the three major South Asian vernaculars spoken widely in Britain - Gujarati, Punjabi and Bengali) was to be further reduced after 1982, and there was already almost none at 'A' level.

Apart from increasing limitation of choice, the major problem seems to lie much more in the mismatch between the kind of candidate for which many of those exams were originally designed, and the new kind of candidate that we have in mind: children and grandchildren of native speakers of the various languages listed in the table, who are growing up with a partial knowledge of the spoken languages, often in non-standard varieties, and who are learning to read and write the standard languages outside or inside school.

Provision by related bodies

(a) Royal Society of Arts: had in the past conducted exams in at least twelve 'minority' languages, including Arabic, Chinese, 'Hindustani' (sic), Portuguese and Polish, and was considering new developments in the field of exams in minority languages.

(b) Institute of Linguists: 'has always adopted the policy of putting considerable effort into minority language testing and is prepared to accept candidates even if there are only one or two for a particular language'. The Institute's exams, at the lower levels in particular, put a heavy emphasis on practical oral and aural skills, and background knowledge of the countries concerned.

(c) International Baccalaureate: used mainly by schools with an international population, this organisation has experience of examining a very wide range of languages. The list current in 1981 of 64 included Arabic, Turkish, Chinese, Polish, Portuguese, Bengali, Gujarati, Hindi, Urdu, Modern Greek, Yoruba and Vietnamese. A large number of the candidates taking these languages were, to some degree, bilingual or trilingual.

Developments in late 1981

(1) The Schools Council published the report on its September 1981 Conference: Examining in a Multicultural Society, which included discussion of language exams. The Council also included consideration of the development of new exams in ethnic minority languages in the new 16+ context as part of its Programme 5 for 1981-83. (See reference in Introduction to this collection.)

(2)   On possible future developments, one of the Boards most closely
      concerned wrote:

      'The question of rationalising the provision of GCE exams in
      minority languages was discussed initially by the Secretaries
      of the Boards at one of their regular meetings. It was agreed
      that the matter was one for the Boards most closely concerned
      to resolve and there have subsequently been some contacts bet-
      ween London, JMB and the Oxford Delegacy. No clear proposals
      have yet been formulated, but it seems likely that there will
      be no radical reorganisation. What will probably happen is that
      the grossly uneconomic duplication of syllabuses in the same
      language will be eliminated, so that eventually each language
      will be examined by one Board alone; the 'borrowing' system
      will ensure that all the languages currently offered will still
      be available for candidates entered through any of the Boards.
      The status of minority languages as subjects in the proposed
      common 16+ exam is unclear. In the absence of any directives on
      the matter from a higher authority, the four regional groups of
      GCE and CSE Boards will presumably provide minority language
      exams in response to demand for them from schools in their
      areas (much as the CSE Boards do at present), although there
      may be scope for establishing a national system of 'borrowing'
      between regions, like the one operated by the GCE Boards.'

(3)   The Oxford Delegacy informed its Centres in November 1981 that
      it was ceasing to provide its own exams in certain of its
      'specially-approved languages' after 1982. The table earlier in
      this section indicates the five languages in our list which are
      affected: it will be noted that in all cases the languages were
      available for borrowing from other Boards, but of course the
      decision did further reduce the choice of syllabus available.

      The Delegacy's letter indicates the reason for this
      contraction:

      'The decision to discontinue the Delegacy's examinations in
      these languages is based on economic considerations. The GCE
      boards, in common with other bodies which are dependent on
      public funds, have become increasingly conscious of the need to
      achieve financial economies in their operations, and the
      viability of examinations with small entries has come under
      particularly close scrutiny. The provision of minority langu-
      ages examinations has developed haphazardly with little co-or-
      dination between the boards, and there was a clear argument for
      rationalising the position in cases where two or more boards
      examined the same language separately for small numbers of
      candidates. The logical course of action was for the Delegacy
      to withdraw its examination in such cases, since the other
      boards' entries for these subjects were significantly larger.'

Table 1: GCE Entries in Minority Languages: University of London: GCE Board: (summer only) 'Specially Approved Languages'*

Advanced Level

Subject Number and Title/Centre Group	'78	'79	'80
703 Classical Arabic Total	43	39	29
704 Classical Armenian Total	1	-	2
707 Bulgarian Total	2	6	2
709 Chinese Total	137	138	201
710 Czech Total	4	2	-
711 Danish Total	7	3	6
712 Dutch Total	57	48	50
715 Modern Greek Total	267	231	233
718 Classical Hebrew Total	33	43	53
719 Modern Hebrew Total	30	26	34
720 Hindi Total	25	18	30
721 Hungarian Total	4	3	5
723 Japanese Total	33	35	44
729 Norwegian Total	7	9	5
731 Classical Persian Total	164	134	88
732 Polish Total	137	88	126
733 Portuguese Total	31	33	42
736 Sanskrit Total	1	2	1
737 Serbo-Croat Total	14	14	12
742 Swahili Total	5	6	11
743 Swedish Total	24	18	15
746 Turkish Total	57	57	62
748 Urdu Total	52	63	67

Ordinary Level

Ordinary Level	'78	'79	'80
702 Amharic	6	13	7
703 Classical Arabic	217	217	219
704 Armenian	24	30	28
706 Bengali	-	-	18
708 Burmese	7	1	2
709 Chinese	821	1117	1344
711 Danish	26	28	43
715 Modern Greek	372	303	350
716 Gujarati	129	90	122
718 Classical Hebrew	143	215	196
719 Modern Hebrew	124	120	121
720 Hindi	103	108	144
723 Japanese	43	48	78
726 Malay	227	236	335
727 Maltese	-	1	2
729 Norwegian	46	27	35
731 Persian	791	806	1002
732 Polish	184	181	220
733 Portuguese	101	103	122
738 Siamese	31	48	58
742 Swahili	30	26	28
743 Swedish	49	48	41
744 Tamil	18	10	7
746 Turkish	125	141	136
748 Urdu	162	161	212

* These figures, for both 'O' and 'A' level, are for candidates entered under UK Regulations, i.e. UK centres and a small number of British Forces Schools and British Schools Overseas.

Table 2: GCE Entries in Minority Languages: summer 1981:
Oxford Delegacy of Local Examinations

ORDINARY LEVEL	OLE centres		other GCE boards								TOTAL
	home	o'seas	AEB	Camb	JMB	Lond	O&C	SUJB	WJEC	N.I.	
Afrikaans	6	–	–	7	3	7	–	–	–	1	25
Amharic	1	–	–	1	–	–	–	–	–	–	2
Arabic (Classical)	11	4	–	10	–	–	–	–	–	–	25
Arabic (Modern)	68	16	12	15	5	6	7	–	2	–	131
Armenian	6	–	–	1	1	–	2	–	–	–	10
Chinese	94	–	1	41	–	–	15	–	–	–	151
Danish	4	–	–	9	–	–	–	–	–	–	13
Dutch	50	42	16	32	14	75	52	1	–	–	282
Greek (Modern)	184	1	1	14	–	–	4	–	–	–	204
Hebrew (Modern)	4	–	–	3	–	–	1	–	–	–	8
Hindi	2	–	–	9	–	–	–	–	–	–	11
Hungarian	4	–	–	–	1	1	–	–	–	–	6
Irish	–	20	–	1	–	42	3	–	–	–	66
Latvian	–	–	–	–	3	2	–	–	–	–	5
Maltese	2	242	–	2	–	–	–	–	–	–	246
Norwegian	10	–	–	10	–	–	1	–	–	–	21
Persian	106	6	4	58	–	–	14	–	–	–	188
Polish	51	–	1	16	–	–	–	–	–	–	68
Portuguese	17	–	–	16	10	–	7	–	3	–	53
Serbo-Croat	9	1	2	7	8	10	–	–	–	–	37
Siamese (Thai)	4	–	–	–	–	–	1	–	–	–	5
Sinhalese	2	–	–	–	–	2	–	–	–	–	4
Swahili	8	–	–	–	–	–	1	–	–	–	9
Swedish	14	2	–	9	–	–	–	–	–	–	25
Turkish	10	5	1	8	–	–	–	–	–	–	24
Urdu	14	–	9	3	–	–	–	–	1	–	27
Vietnamese	15	–	–	–	–	3	–	–	–	–	18
Yoruba	8	–	–	–	–	3	1	–	1	–	13

ADVANCED LEVEL	OLE centres		other GCE boards				TOTAL
	home	overseas	AEB	Camb	O&C	WJEC	
Arabic (Classical)	4	–	–	2	1	–	7
Dutch	3	26	–	2	–	1	32
Persian (Classical)	13	1	1	3	7	–	25
Polish	8	–	1	–	–	–	9

Table 3: GCE Entries in Minority Languages 1978-81:
Joint Matriculation Board

	1978	1979	1980	1981
Polish (O)	133	148	131	128
Ukrainian (O)	37	46	38	41
Punjabi (O)	94	115	93	202
Modern Hebrew (O)	32	28	41	38
Punjabi (A)	-	-	6	9
Modern Hebrew (A)	6	8	7	6

Table 4: 'Borrowing' of Papers in Minority Languages

University of London: GCE Board:
O level language papers borrowed from other Boards

Language	Summer 78	Summer 79	Summer 80	Borrowed from
Afrikaans	8	7	5	Oxford
Dutch	24	49	37	"
Hungarian	5	8	3	"
Irish	5	103	104	N. Ireland
Irish	39	41	46	Oxford
Latvian	1	1	2	"
Modern Arabic	2	10	3	"
Modern Hebrew	31	49	47	Oxford & Camb
Modern Standard Chinese	1	3	-	Cambridge
Punjabi	7	18	46	JMB
Serbo-Croat	6	4	3	Oxford
Sinhalese	2	2	3	"
Ukrainian	4	9	8	JMB
Vietnamese	-	1	-	Oxford
Welsh	-	4	-	Welsh
Yoruba	-	5	2	Oxford

Table 4: 'Borrowing' of Papers in Minority Languages continued

Oxford Local: GCE Board:
Language Papers Borrowed from other Boards, Summer 1981

O Levels

Bengali	2 (overseas candidates)
Gujarati	4 (home candidates)
Japanese	3 (home candidates)
Malay	21 (home candidates)
Ukrainian	1 (home candidate)

A Levels

Chinese	8 (home)
Danish	1 (overseas)
Modern Greek	31 (home)
Modern Hebrew	2 (overseas)
Hungarian	1 (home)
Japanese	3 (home)
Norwegian	1 (overseas)
Portuguese	1 (home)
Serbo-Croat	1 (overseas)
Swedish	1 (overseas)
Turkish	2 (home)

Ukrainian borrowed from JMB; all others from London.

Recommendations

The Working Party's recommendations on availability are to be found in part II of their Report - Section A of this collection.

CURRENCY

This section of the paper is based on a circular enquiry sent in June 1981 to the Admissions Officers and Registrars of all UK universities, polytechnics in England, Wales and Northern Ireland, and to equivalent institutions in Scotland. The questions posed were as follows:

(1) For what range of courses in your institution are examination passes in languages other than English required?

(2) For any such courses do you distinguish, in terms of the languages you find acceptable, between:
- (a) the languages at present most commonly taught in UK schools – French, German, Spanish, Italian, Russian, Latin, Classical Greek – and
- (b) other languages which may have close associations with minority communities in the UK – e.g. Arabic, Bengali, Chinese, Hindi, Gujarati, Modern Greek, Punjabi, Polish, Turkish, Ukrainian, Urdu, Yoruba?

(3) Do you make a distinction between applicants offering any of the languages mentioned above as 'foreign languages', or as 'mother tongues'? If so, on what basis do you determine for a particular applicant what status the language has?

(4) Do you have any analysis available of the extent to which languages listed in 2b above have been offered or accepted as part of entrance requirements in recent years?

Responses were received from twelve of the Polytechnics, and four HE institutions in Scotland as follows:
Brighton, Coventry (Lanchester), Hatfield (from four different departments), Kingston, Leeds, Leicester, Liverpool, Oxford, Portsmouth, Teeside, Wales, Wolverhampton; Dundee College of Technology, Paisley College of Technology, Scottish College of Textiles, Duncan of Jordanstone College of Art.

A further 36 replies were received from university institutions:
Aston (three departments); Birmingham, Bradford, Brunel, Cambridge, Durham (two departments), East Anglia, Essex, Exeter, Hull, Keele, Lancaster, Leicester (two departments), London: Senate House and Bedford, Birkbeck, Chelsea, Imperial, LSE, UC; Newcastle, Oxford, Salford, Southamptom, Surrey. Sussex, Warwick (two departments), Wales: Aberystwyth, Cardiff, Swansea; Dundee, Heriot– Watt, Scottish Universities Council on Entrance (for Glasgow); Joint Matriculation Board, UCCA.

Responses from Polytechnics and Colleges

Question 1: In all cases in this group of institutions, passes in languages other than English were only specifically required for entry to those courses which were wholly or partly concerned with the study of modern languages – which did not in any of the responding institutions include non-European languages.

However, in terms of the general entrance requirement for degree courses, in England and Wales usually specified as five GCE passes of which two must be at 'A' level, assuming that the applicant satisfies the special entry requirements for the course, and had the necessary English language qualifications, then the number of passes might be made up by one in another language.

Question 2: Formally, the general position seemed to be that all exams approved by GCE Boards have equal status in terms of satisfying general entrance requirements. However, since admissions decisions are in effect taken by individual course tutors in the various faculties and departments, there is extensive scope for the exercise of individual judgement. Some extracts from the responses received will indicate the range of attitudes forming such judgements:

From a Languages and European Studies Department in the west midlands referring to the languages listed in Question 2b: 'These languages are not subjects of study here so passes in them are not relevant'.
From a northern Admissions Office '...it would be unlikely that the other languages (i.e. those listed in Question 2b) would be found unacceptable'.
From an Academic Secretariat in the south midlands '...every applicant is in competition...course tutors are bound to take into account...how effective as a test of the applicant's academic ability the subject was. In this connection the admitting course tutor is likely to take the view that an 'A' level in the applicant's mother tongue should be easier to obtain than the same 'A' level for an applicant whose mother tongue was, say, English'.
From an Academic Registry in the north-west: '...would not expect any discrimination between the more traditional languages and the languages more commonly associated with minorities in the UK.'
From an Civil Engineering Division in London: '...would not discriminate against a potential student offering an 'O' level pass in his native tongue if it were not English. On a personal basis I have been uneasy about this situation for some time, as it seems a very easy option. It must be very easy to pass an examination set at a very low level, as a foreign language, in one's own native language. Certainly the standard required would be very much lower than that required in English Language for English students'.
From the northern Admissions Office again: 'It seems reasonable to expect that prospective teachers with these qualifications would be valuable assets to schools in areas with immigrant populations'.
From Language & Area Studies Department in the south: 'Passes in minority languages are useful in showing a candidate's linguistic ability and would form part of his general academic profile'.

Question 3: With one exception, the answer to the first part of this question was a straightforward 'no': i.e. it was claimed that no distinction was made between applicants offering the languages mentioned as 'foreign languages' or 'mother tongues'. The exception was a tutor in an Engineering Department, who said: 'Yes. I do not accept, say, Persian 'O' level and TOFEL'. (sic).

Question 4: No-one had any systematic analysis available, but two made impressionistic comments: '...minority language most commonly offered is Chinese, by students living in the UK only for educational purposes' and '...despite increasing numbers of applications from ethnic and cultural minorities...we do not have many cases of students offering these languages as alternatives to any other subjects which might have been thought more suitable...a large number of applicants from Iran, or Iranians settled here, offer this language at 'O' level....however, they all appear to offer so many other subjects which make it unlikely for us to have to make a decision as to whether or not Persian is acceptable'.

Response from Universities

Question 1: As for the Polytechnics, it is necessary to distinguish between specific course requirements, generally expressed in terms of 'A' levels, and general entry requirements, expressed as a combination of 'A' level and 'O' level, (or Scottish Higher and Ordinary Grades). As far as the former are concerned, passes in languages were seen as relevant only when they themselves, or related disciplines such as literature, history or archeology, were to be the subjects of study.

For general entry requirements, only Oxford and Cambridge seemed to demand a language other than English from all applicants, no matter which subject they wish to follow. A number of other universities, such as Exeter, required a foreign language for all applicants to their Arts Faculty, and it was quite common for would-be students of history, English literature, music and art in the universities to be asked for a pass at 'O' level in a language additional to English.

Question 2: The answers to this question varied, as it did in the Polytechnic responses. Prospectuses, and Registrars, made it clear that a pass in 'any approved language' – meaning in practice any of the languages examined by GCE or SCE Boards – was in principle acceptable as part of the general entry requirement. For example:

- Cambridge: 'We do not distinguish between the two groups of languages....'
- London (University Entrance Requirements Division): 'Languages which have a close association with the minority communities in the UK are certainly regarded as suitable subjects towards the satisfaction of our general entrance requirements.'
- Durham (Oriental Studies): 'Most languages would...be regarded as valid in indicating a candidate's general linguistic ability, provided only that there was overall confidence both in the method of teaching and in the standard of the examinations.'

- <u>LSE</u>: 'Any modern foreign language may be offered at 'O' level for candidates for the BA history degree.... For example, a student... with a Cypriot background...can offer Modern Greek as the foreign language requirement.'
- <u>Joint Matriculation Board</u> (which determines the general entrance requirement for the Universities of Manchester, Liverpool, Leeds, Sheffield and Birmingham): '...all of the languages mentioned in your letter, paragraph 2, both A & B would be considered acceptable subjects.'
- <u>Scottish Universities Council on Entrance</u> (which has responsibility for drawing up the list of subjects approved for purposes of the general entrance requirements of the Scottish universities): From the list in question 2b, at present Arabic, Chinese, Modern Greek, Polish and Turkish are acceptable, but, 'The basis of acceptability of languages other than English is at present under review.' (<u>Dundee</u> adds that this consultation is about '... the extension of this list to include all languages in which GCE papers are offered.')

However, there were qualifications made of two basic kinds. Firstly, and more commonly, were those which indicate a strong preference, or even a requirement, that there should be an obvious and direct link between the course applied for and the language offered. For example:

- <u>Oxford</u>: 'A knowledge of certain oriental languages (e.g. Arabic, Chinese, Egyptian, Hebrew, Japanese, Persian, Sanskrit, Turkish) might be an advantage for a candidate intending to read Oriental Studies....'
- <u>Leicester</u> (Classical Studies): 'Indo-European languages connected with Ancient Greek and Latin would be preferred, e.g. the languages listed in 2a + Modern Greek, Polish and Ukrainian, and in second place the languages of North India, Bangladesh and Pakistan'.
- <u>London, Imperial College</u>: With reference to the 4-year Engineering Degree, which includes a modern language component: '... the languages of the 'minority communities' which you list under 2b would not normally be acceptable, since we are looking, basically, for a 'commercial' language.' '...the requirement is for a 'modern' foreign language - which will generally be French or German, but may be, say, Russian, Spanish or possibly Italian. Students on the course are normally requires to follow one of these languages for at least one or two years...'
- <u>Sussex</u>: 'We will only accept modern European languages as evidence of ability in languages for these courses' (i.e. courses offered in French, Russian, German, Italian and Classics).

The second type of qualification often indicated a degree of doubt about passes in the languages occurring in list 2b, some feeling that they might have been 'easy options', and that it was natural therefore to expect higher grades than those that might be acceptable from the list 2a languages. For example:

126

- <u>Bradford</u>: 'Languages listed in your question 2b are almost always taken by native speakers, from whom we would expect better grades in any qualifications....'
<u>Wales (Aberystwyth)</u>: '...we would treat with some caution cases where candidates were offering GCE qualifications in 'foreign' languages when it was clear that the candidates had 'mother tongue' fluency...we would be specially careful in our assessment of a candidate's academic ability if this sort of thing happened....'
- <u>Surrey</u> (Department of Linguistic and International Studies): 'People who have ('0' level passes in Polish) are almost always of Polish extraction. They often have an oral knowledge of the language, which is not supported by any systematic knowledge of the grammar and the written language. In some cases the knowledge of the language they have can be outweighed by the bad linguistic habits into which they have fallen through the unsystematic manner in which they learnt. This, incidentally, can be a problem with so-called 'bilinguals': they never obtain a completely disciplined and 'educated' command of one or even both of the languages.'

<u>Question 3</u>: Most responses claimed that no distinction was made between languages offered as 'foreign languages' or as 'mother tongues'. Of those who did make the distinction, <u>London's</u> University Entrance Requirements Division offered the most explicit basis – medium of education. 'A candidate who has been educated in the medium of English can count one of these languages as a foreign language. If, however, his education was not conducted in English, he will be able to count English as a foreign language.' <u>Bradford</u>, <u>Hull</u> and <u>Sussex</u> all refer to the interview, and <u>Bradford</u> alone to the UCCA form as the source of information for deciding what status the language has for the individual, but do not explain what criteria they use nor what consequence their decision has for the evaluation of the qualification.

<u>Sussex</u>, however, does indicate that '...a good grade in a mother tongue does not compensate for a very poor grade in other subject'; and <u>Surrey</u> again comments that '... the candidate with an '0' level of this kind (generally) has taken that '0' level because it is the language spoken at home though not at school.... Too often candidates finish up with no command of either language'. <u>Durham's</u> Oriental Studies course appears to be alone in explicitly refusing speakers of some of the languages listed in our question 2b: 'As a matter of principle, native speakers are not admitted to courses in Modern Arabic, Persian or Turkish, though Arabic speakers may study Classical Arabic. No restriction is made in the case of Chinese, in that the languages taught (Standard Modern Chinese and Classical Chinese) are so far removed from the Cantonese generally spoken by immigrants from Hong Kong. The main criterion used to identify 'native speakers' of Arabic, Persian or Turkish, is the language of

secondary education, though a pupil at school in England but returning for most of the holidays to an entirely native-speaking environment would be classed in the same way'.

Question 4: No statistics were available from any of the institutions responding, although Southampton offered the possibility of extracting the information from their computer. LSE believed the numbers to be so small that an analysis of them would be of little value.

Once again, then, we were offered only a number of impressions:

- Cambridge: '...we are not infrequently asked to approve a qualification in one of the languages listed in 2b...not necessarily GCE. Mostly, but not always, these requests are on behalf of people educated abroad rather than in the UK, though some of their schooling may have been here'.
- Keele: '...of those listed, we have certainly had moderate numbers in recent years offering Arabic, Chinese, Gujarati, Modern Greek, Polish amd Turkish'.
- London, Imperial: '...a fair number of our students who are overseas nationals offer 'O' levels in other languages — primarily because they are their 'mother tongues'. The most common...are Arabic, Chinese and Greek'.
- Sussex: '...we have accepted a number with Arabic and Modern Greek, a smaller number with Chinese, and one or two with Polish'.
- Warwick (Italian Department): 'We often have applicants from Italian communities in Britain, whom we welcome'.
- Dundee: 'My impression would be that only Chinese of the languages, mentioned in...2b, has been offered in significant numbers in recent years...and that students offering this language were Hong Kong- based rather than UK residents'.

Recommendations

The Working Party's recommendations on the currency of these examinations are contained in Part II of their Report — Section A of this collection.

*   This paper is a compilation from material submitted to the Working Party on The Languages of Minority Communities during 1981 and the author gladly acknowledges the very full co-operation of the examination boards and related bodies.

Section C: Some Examples of Practice

TEACHING GUJARATI AT ALPERTON HIGH SCHOOL*

Hasmukh Patel**
Community Language (formerly 'Mother Tongue') Project

PROMOTING COMMUNITY LANGUAGES IN SECONDARY SCHOOLS

There are very many ways in which individual schools can do more to recognise the linguistic resouces already possessed by their students. Self-confidence, a real pride in one's culture, incentives to reach out for all kinds of new knowledge, all of these can be generated in adolescents through a more positive deployment of the skills of existing staff, and through the greater involvement of local linguistic communities in the life of a school. Although a long-term financial commitment is of course necessary for a proper realisation of the potential, it has to be said that much of the most useful innovation which has occurred in secondary schools in Britain has so far been achieved with little or no funding. The Alperton High School Community Language Project exemplifies this trend. The economic situtation of the country and of individual local authorities cannot be seen as the sole reasons for past failure to maximise the benefits which accrue from a multilingual population.

A document composited by John Broadbent and Nicola Povey of the Brent Language Service provides a checklist of some of the enriching possibilities that have been implemented in various schools through-out the country. (See the Questionnaire in the Appendix 2). The major achievement at Alperton so far has taken place within the curriculum itself. Gujarati has been introduced to the school's timetable within a frame-work which gives the language parity of status with German as an option open to all from the third year to a school-leaving exam at CSE of 'O' level. Unlike many of the reports that have become available on the introduction of mother tongue teaching in particular and on the reform of language education in general, this is an account of how innovation came to be introduced from below, and how teachers, then School Governors, then the local Education Committee came to be convinced by the arguments and the practice of the Project described.

FACTORS FAVOURING DEVELOPMENTS AT ALPERTON

It would admittedly have been much more difficult to succeed without the far-sighted staffing policy and the system of devolved management introduced by the Headteacher. Her positive encouragement for the Project and for multicultural education has proved invaluable. The previous Headteacher, who retired in 1977, summed up the school's attitude to mother-tongue maintenance thus: 'We were not in favour of the policy of teaching non-European first languages in school time. Traditionally it has been the responsibility of the minority communities themselves to organise instruction on their own languages.' Books were however made available in the school library in languages other than English, facilities were provided for sitting the exams in specially approved languages set by London University School Examinations Department, and in some contexts pupils were encouraged to use Creoles and other home languages for literary purposes.

One of the major innovations which followed the arrival of a new Headteacher was the reorganisation of the Parent Teacher Association. Given that the main function of the PTA at Alperton is to look after the interests of pupils in each year group in the school, it was felt that a proper representation could only be achieved through the election of twelve parents on to the committee, two for each year group from the parents of children of the relevant ages. This expansion of the PTA immediately brought its composition more into line with the racial composition of the school as a whole. Although the PTA as a body remained in broad sympathy with the introduction of Gujarati into the curriculum along the lines outlined in this paper, it has to be admitted that there has not perhaps been sufficient involvement of parents in the design and teaching of the course.

The 1944 Education Act does provide the institutional channels for determining the kind of education which schools should provide in order 'to meet the needs of the population of ther area'. The decisions of Governing Bodies can in fact override Local Education Authority policy in almost all matters except finance. It is moreover a unique historical feature of the education system in England that individual schools and Local Education Authorities are relatively independent of government interference at the level of curricular policy. The Department of Education and Science drew attention to the decentralised nature of the English system as one reason for weakening the force of the Directive, drafted in 1975 by the European Commission, on the education of the children of migrant workers with special reference to their need of instruction in the mother tongue and culture of the country of origin. The draft was amended to meet the objections expressed by the DES and came into force as a binding Directive in July 1981. For the purposes of funding the EC Commission has, in a letter from the Director General for Research, Science and Education, declared the Alperton Project to be 'fully in line' with the above Directive. No financial assistance has however been sought beyond the local authority, and none granted over and above the normal school capitation.

The Project operating at Alperton High School sees as a central aim the mutual enrichment of the diverse linguistic communities that currently compose the student population, rather than the possibility of their reintegration into the states of origin as envisaged by the Directive.

Our practice has been usefully informed by the cautiously expressed evidence of two research projects based at the University of London Institute of Education — one run by Rosen and Burgess (1980), the other by the Linguistic Minorities Project — as well as of Pilot Projects supported by the EC. Most central to our concerns and to those of parents involved has been the unequivocal statement from the European Commission (1978) that:

> 'in normal classes, tuition in the language and culture of origin contributes towards the cognitive development and socialization of immigrant children in so far as such tuition forms an integral part of the school syllabus.'

There is no published evidence as yet of any pupils held back in their schooling through exposure within the normal timetable to the languages of their respective communities. Such provision is moreover totally consistent with the 1944 Education Act in so far as that Act places an obligation on LEAs and on the Governing Bodies of schools to service the needs of their local population. It is important to stress that first and foremost schools have a responsibility to provide adequate support in those forms of language generally required for social and occupational purposes, namely in English. It is however valid to point out that any student who leaves school unable to function in more than one language has in fact been deprived of the additional cognitive and emotional exposure that State education ought to entail.

Modern languages continue to occupy a strong position within educational priorities for the compulsory years of schooling between the ages of eleven and sixteen. In a typical arrangement for comprehensive schools, French is part of a core curriculum at Alperton for the first three years from eleven upwards, and German is offered as an option to thirteen-year-olds. For partly geographical, partly historical reasons French has pride of place as the most commonly taught living language in British secondary schools. This situation tends to reproduce itself in terms of the resources both human and material which are available, and exercises a restrictive effect upon the range of language options. To the prime-movers of our Project it seemed likely that class participation and motivation could be enormously improved in modern languages if we selected forms of speech and writing in which some students already possessed extended knowledge. If it is agreed that all children should learn at least one language besides their mother tongue it is then logical to aim at some level of bilingualism in schools where positive local attitudes permit. Once the issues were presented in this light, it appeared that Gujarati, Urdu and Hindi amongst other locally used languages might turn out to be just as productive for educational purposes as is French.

Probably the major impetus for change in this direction at Alperton has been provided by the students themselves, through the open debates, the Asian film shows and the social occasions which they have confidently organised over several years. The Gujarati community around the school is particularly cohesive, with a widely circulated newspaper, a broad range of cultural organisations, some of which offer mother tongue classes, and a political network which extends into the local Council and into the Governing Bodies of the State schools. By and large our students reflect the optimistic dynamism so much in evidence in the diverse communities that have settled in and around Alperton, although some, as will be mentioned below, have displayed a reluctance to declare that they are familiar with any language other than English.

FIRST STEPS

The first evidence of staff involvement in the issues inherent in a multilingual environment dates from the publication in July 1979 of a Brent Teachers' Centre discussion document entitled 'Bilingualism in Brent Schools'. Two teachers from Alperton High School had taken part for more than a year in a working party set up by the Multiracial Panel at the Teachers' Centre: they had discussed the implications of 'a vast increase over the previous decade in the number of pupils in the Borough whose native tongue is not English.' Clearly there was a need to define the issues more precisely by discovering what languages, what numbers of pupils and what levels of competence were involved. On the basis of reliable statistics rather than intuitive impressions it would become clearer which particular languages it might become possible to promote in the school environment.

The damage to the self-image of pupils who at home speak Gujarati or any language other than English is amply demonstrated by the reluctance of some of them to speak their language in school, or even to admit to their knowledge of it for the purposes of our School Survey on the range of mother-tongues present in Alperton High School. One student even stated that prior to the Survey she did not realise that the way they spoke at home was a proper language. Altogether 1015 students out of a total of 1444 were surveyed by their form teachers using the questionnaire enclosed in Appendix 2 of this chapter; it proved impossible to secure the support of the entire pastoral staff for our unofficial venture. For this reason, and because a number of students were shy about revealing the language spoken in the home, the figures obtained on the incidence of various community languages in the school's population are likely to be lower than the real situation.

When particular languages were shown to exist as mother tongues amongst the pupils, attempts were then made to discover how many members of staff might become competent to teach them bilingually. Eighty-nine teachers out of just over a hundred spoke English as a mother tongue at that time, as compared to less than seven hundred out of just over a thousand students. Approximately one third of the student population had some knowledge of Gujarati, whilst not one member of staff could use it fluently. If the ratio of members of a particular speech community were to be proportional for staff and pupils alike we would have needed a total of twenty-three teachers speaking Gujarati. There were incidentally five teachers claiming a high level of competence in spoken French, but only one child was a native speaker of a French-based Creole, and none had access outside of school hours to contexts where standard French was a normal means of communication. This fairly typical mismatch has been offset to some extent by recent appointments, but may well have contributed to the collective feeling of unease that the linguistic needs of the school population were not being met any more adequately than the linguistic resources were being exploited.

The Brent Bilingual Working Party had recommended in 1979 that mother tongues should be offered as a modern language option in secondary schools. At that time Aylestone High School was alone in the Borough in offering a two-year course in Gujarati to native speakers: that school had, in addition, received support from the London Regional Examining Board for its own Mode 3 CSE exam in Gujarati. Hostile critics argued that such practices would operate against the integration of ethnic minorities and would impede progress in learning English. The juxtaposition by detractors of the wide range of languages identified and the shortage of funds and qualified teachers reflected closely some of the arguments advanced by the DES in opposing the 1975 Draft Directive of the European Commission. The statistics obtained at Alperton did tend to suggest that it would be unrealistic for the school to offer Swahili, Dutch, Japanese, Ga, Nepali, Cantonese and Tamil to the solitary native speakers of those languages, unless peripatetic teachers could be employed. Such provision should not be beyond the bounds of possibility to service the minority communities which exist in greater numbers in other parts of Brent, using Italian, Polish, Spanish, Chinese, Bengali amongst others. The remaining statistics in the Alperton Survey of significant groups who were receiving no instruction for literacy in their various languages prompted the setting up of out of school classes in Gujarati, Hindi and Urdu. Initially the classes were funded by the Youth Club, but this support was withdrawn by the Director of Education in line with an Education Committee decision on finance.

A number of difficult questions were facing the teachers involved. Even more important than the attitude of the Education Committee and of critical colleagues, what was the attitude of parents towards our

133

Project? The very act of making a survey of the languages already present in the school population, for which parental permission was sought as a matter of course, had generated a fair degree of enthusiasm amongst the students and their parents for the more systematic learning of the various mother tongues. Proceeding with the due caution recommended in the discussion document circulated by the Brent Bilingual Working Party (1979) we asked ourselves whether there was in the Community sufficient acceptance of multicultural education in general. The Working Party's document had suggested that 'other cultures must become an accepted part of school life before other languages can. If minority students are helped to a more positive view of their own culture they will develop more desire to foster their own tongue instead of feeling ashamed and secretive about it, as many now do.' We in the Project at Alperton remained convinced that until languages like Gujarati, Hindi, Punjabi and Urdu were integrated into the normal range of options in schools like our own, the users of those languages would continue to consider them as second rate. We had to start somewhere.

We produced a trilingual letter for parents and students (see Appendix 1 to this chapter) to determine how much interest there would be for extracurricular provision, with the perspective that once a certain amount of expertise had been gained we would have a better case for bringing the languages into the curriculum. We were very excited to see that amongst the hundred or so students who volunteered for lessons there were some of Jamaican origin and others born in this country of West Indian, English and Irish parents: we did our best to encourage their interest. Of those who spoke one or other of the languages as a mother tongue we were surprised to see how few could write the language spoken at home. We agreed as a result that writing and reading skills would be a central focus in our work. We also agreed that since the students were sacrificing their leisure time, the activities offered in the classes should be broadly recreational. This decision had important repercussions as far as the methodologies evolved for teaching literacy in alphabets other than Roman.

With the full approval of the school's Governing Body which had met to discuss 'Biligualism in Brent Schools' a full description of our Project was written up for inclusion on the Register of European Research filed at the Centre for Information on Language Teaching. At that time the stated aims were:

1. to develop a standardised approach in the adaptation of materials used for the more commonly taught languages such as English, French and German to the needs of minority mother tongue teaching;

2. to evaluate published teaching materials for Gujarati, Hindi and Urdu;

3. to establish a workshop aimed at solving problems of materials and teaching methodology for those involved in mother tongue teaching;

4. to identify the obstacles impeding the teaching of mother tongues within the school timetable, and to discover ways of overcoming those obstacles.

A special meeting of the Parent Teachers' Association for the school was convened at which we described our progress to date. A resolution presented from the floor and agreed without dissension recommended that 'Alperton should press ahead with its multicultural initiatives with all possible resources whilst recognizing that this must not be to the detriment of the host language and culture'.

GUJARATI IN THE TIMETABLE

It was becoming more generally admitted that voluntary classes of the kind we were operating did not go far enough in improving the status of minority languages within the school. Only their inclusion as an option in the normal school timetable could begin to do that. Initially in an ad hoc curriculum forum, then on the school's Management Committee and finally in the Governing Body where the arguments were aired successively it was agreed that Gujarati should become an option in the school timetable from September 1981, for any third year students who were interested, regardless of their linguistic background. It was later agreed that tuition in Urdu for students in the fourth year, and in the lower sixth could take place in assembly time before school. These decisions represented an enormous step forward for the Project. Capitation became available and it was possible to envisage the production on the school's offset litho press of teaching materials able to bear comparison with those used for European languages in terms of interest and attractiveness.

The information about the proposed Gujarati course which was circulated to second year students and their parents prior to September 1981 read as follows:

'This course is open to all students, whether you know some Gujarati or not. Those of you who are new to the language should learn enough during the year to allow you to take part in simple everyday coversations in a variety of situations, with Gujarati-speaking friends. You will all learn how to read and write the Gujarati script - which is different from that used in English. The lessons will be based around topics such as 'food' 'telling the time' 'the family' and 'school'. Those interested in the subject will be able to follow a course in your 4th and 5th years leading to either an 'O' level or CSE examination.'

Twenty-two students volunteered for the course beginning in September 1981. A significant number of them were found not to speak Gujarati at home. Their presence was especially welcome for social reasons in that they prevented Gujarati from being seen as a 'ghetto' option, although they presented methodological problems which are still not fully solved. Whilst the numbers of students staying with the course after one year have approximately halved, Gujarati is now a firm language option in the school, with the numbers opting to begin in September 1982 being almost double those of the previous year.

STAFF DEVELOPMENT

A Report on the teaching of Gujarati at Alperton High School would not be complete without a genuine tribute to those who have supported our Project voluntarily and without payment. The Head of English at Alperton High School for example undertook a term-long visit to the Gujarati, where she studied the language and the available teaching methods. The hours which other teachers have put into designing materials, into discussing methods and into the practical teaching of the languages in which they are competent, are in themselves ample proof that teachers and resources are not as difficult to obtain as has often been claimed. Indeed if LEAs and the institutions existing for the training of teachers had taken seriously the DES Report (1971) which heralded the presence of 'Commonwealth immigrant pupils' as a great educational resource for State schools, they would have had ample time by now to have attracted from abroad, and trained here, sufficient numbers of teachers in all the languages spoken by community groups in the UK. A decade is surely long enough to train a person to teach their native language; the fact that no genuine attempt seems ever to have been made has led to our situation in Alperton where bilingual teachers like the present author are trying - with a fair amount of success - to acquire appropriate pedagogical techniques through trial and error.

Such an important area of language education cannot continue for long to be supported solely by the commitment and expertise of a few willing teachers. A proper policy on the place of community languages in State schools has to be evolved, and a proper career structure provided to support the policy reached. The efforts made in various inner-city schools to reform the language curriculum deserve to receive wider publicity and central financing if valuable initiatives are not to be lost. At Alperton High School we are experiencing extreme difficulty in finding the time to document our discoveries. In order to disseminate these discoveries, many of which we believe to be of more than local significance, we need the services of a research worker at the very least. Until such support is made available the compilation of further reports of this nature will be almost impossible.

*   This Report was commissioned for the July 1982 Assembly of NCLE.

**   The author joined the staff of Alperton High School in 1980 as a
       member of its science Department. He is one of a tem of three
       teachers who have developed a syllabus for Gujarati in the
       school, combining a strategy fro mother tongue maintenance with
       the elaboration of language learning objectives which can be met
       by students for whom Gujarati is not the home language.

APPENDIX 1: LETTER TO PARENTS AND STUDENTS

VOLUNTARY LESSONS IN URDU AND GUJARATI   Alperton High School

Last year a survey was organised to discover how many students at
Alperton can speak more than one language. At that time many people
said that they would like to widen their knowlede of Gujarati or
Urdu: many who can already speak one of the Asian languages wished
to learn to write it.

In the near future we hope to be able to offer out-of-school classes
at Alperton in both Urdu and Gujarati, possibly up to 'O' level. If
you are interested in studying either of them, please fill in the
form below and return it to Mr Broadbent at Ealing Road, or to Mr
Nawathe at Stanley Avenue.

[Urdu and Gujarati translation of the above were printed here]

Name ....Form ....

Choose one language and place a tick beside it: Urdu

                                                       Gujarati
How much of your chosen language do you know already? Tick the
sentences which are true:

I can already understand it   I can already read it

I can already speak it   I can already write it

When would you like the lessons to be? Weekends   After school

---

APPENDIX 2: ALPERTON HIGH SCHOOL LANGUAGE SURVEY

Form teacher .... Form ....

I am asking for your co-operation in determining how many of our students have a first language other than English. When obtaining the information, please emphasise that bi-lingualism is a positive advantage rather than a handicap. The form has spaces for you to note down the names of all students in your class who can speak and/or write Gujarati. If there are any other pupils who speak another language as well as or better than English, please include them in the lower part of the form. Many thanks.

NAME OF STUDENTS   PLEASE TICK APPROPRIATE COLUMNS

brought up speaking Gujerati	able to write mother tongue	receiving tuition in mother tongue	receiving extra tuition in English
1................			
2................			
3................			
4................			
5................			
6................			
7................			
8................			
9................			
10................			
11................			
12................			

brought up speaking any other language other than English or Gujerati	name of language

....
....
....
....
....
....

GROWING UP BILINGUAL: A REPORT

John Wright
Advisory Centre for Education

The poster 'Growing up bilingual' reproduced on pages 144 – 145 was
distributed to schools via advisors/inspectors for multi-ethnic/-
multicultural education in a number of local education authority
areas, including Bradford, Northampton, Berkshire, Haringey and
Inner London.

The poster had two aims. First, to raise awareness amongst teachers
in schools of the issues (in terms of both needs and possibilities)
arising from the presence in our classrooms of bilingual pupils and
students. Second, to discover and document the range of positive
responses which many schools across the country have made to the
multi-lingual nature of the communities they now serve.

Many of the individual teachers, teacher groups and organisations
which responded, did so tentatively. The experiences they sought to
share with other colleagues were offered, not as models of ideal
practice, but as evidence of steps taken along the road of
recognising, utilising and fostering the linguistic skill and understanding possessed by bilingual pupils and students. A summary of
the responses follows.

A primary school reported that teachers had surveyed the reading
habits of all the children in the school. They asked about reading
in the home languages of bilingual pupils and discovered that a
number of children were obtaining books in their home languages from
the local library. Staff had been spurred on by the results of their
survey to acquire books in a variety of languages for the school
library. They plan to buy books which children can read for
themselves and books for children to take home and get a parent or
an older brother or sister to read out to them.

Teachers have made a beginning with translating some of the children's own stories into some of the languages of the community – on
tape and in booklet form.

Occasionally, community languages (in spoken and written form) are
introduced into project work through the school. As yet there is no
central record kept of how and when this is done. Children's
responses have been enthusiastic and staff are keen to monitor this
work and exchange information and experience.

Other schools reported:

- Parents and older children reading stories in community languages for young pupils.

- Books in community languages available for loan in the school library and on sale in the school bookshop.

- Stories and plays in community languages used as part of the school assembly; in particular, well-known stories such as 'Cinderella', where the meaning is obvious to all children.

- Children attending out-of-school voluntary Greek and Turkish classes writing stories in these languages for other pupils in the school to read.

- Mothers, working together with teachers, producing bilingual versions of well-known folk tales.

- School and classroom notices written in community languages and teachers and parents working together to produce the translations.

- Songs in Hebrew, Greek, Turkish, Gujarati and Cantonese taught to the whole school and sung in assembly.

- Parents coming into school to cook traditional dishes - the recipes in English and the relevant community language pinned up on the classroom wall.

- With new entrants, older children, peers, brothers and sisters spending time talking with them each day in their mother-tongue languages.

One primary school reported:

1. We have a teacher who speaks Urdu: with co-operation from colleagues who cover her class, she does a weekly story session for an Infant and a Junior group, of Urdu speakers. She also does home visits to Urdu-speaking families and can sometimes translate for speakers of other dialects who have difficulty with English - especially on occasions like medicals.

2. Where possible, we translate notices for our Parents' Board, and we make good use of the 'Welcome Poster' in various languages produced by Bedfordshire County Council.

3. In our Infant and Junior libraries we include: (a) books written in mother tongue and English; (b) books which are

solely mother-tongue versions of well-known stories; and (c) books written in English but produced by Asian publishing firms.

4. All the teachers encourage individuals to tell the other children **their** words for certain objects, e.g. on the interest table or in handwork, in a very relaxed casual way, not as a class lesson. This often extends to an interest in their own style of writing.

5. We make a positive effort to define which children are bilingual when they first enter school either to the nursery or rising-five class. We then make a point of advising parents to keep up mother-tongue practice; so many seem to feel they should concentrate on English and drop mother tongue in order to help the child when he/she starts school.

6. We encourage mothers to come into the nursery and talk to children in their mother tongue, as we often found that those slow to speak English were also slow in development of their own language, and facility in the one they know best helps the development of the English. Older children in the school help in this way too. (Not as much as we would like here – participation by contact from parents is as yet sparce.)

7. During the year, we have displays and celebrations of festivals of different religions: the displays always include notices in the appropriate language as well as English.

A secondary school offered the following description of a project being undertaken by the teacher of English as a Second Language.

Project Title: <u>Mother-tongue recognition.</u>

<u>Groups</u>

The groups involved were first-, second- and third-year groups of ten – twelve; one group, through new admissions, grew to twenty and had to be split. The levels of competence in English ranged from complete beginners to second-stage learners.

The groups were, in the main, of mixed language-level and mixed ability, so that in any group there would be several fairly fluent children along with some beginners.

The aim

To look at ways in which mother tongue can become a positive factor in school: to use the mother tongue as a way in to learning English, and to expand the range of English used by pupils.

What came out of the project?

(1) Nearly all the children showed that they could tell stories in their mother tongue at a level of sophistication which was fascinating to watch. Many were able spontaneously to draw up a group of peers to them, and to tell the story in a way which was worthy of the story in mode of telling – gesture, repetition, etc.

(2) It was clear that only the most competent translators would be selected by the children to give the English rendition, and that there was much discussion as to the precise translation. A boy who can speak 'survival' English chose to tell the story in his mother tongue, then monitor carefully the translation. The art of translation – to find exactly the right words and phrases in the right rhythms, and to find equivalents of flora and fauna, etc – was very highly valued and the subject of much discussion and searching for the right form of expression, including the art of repetition, word-play, etc.

(3) Thus the stories and illustrations provided a very useful way in to teaching English: initial vocabulary-item utterances could be built up into phrases and eventually a whole story. It involved repetition, including imposed repetition involving Language Masters, and repetition which is organic to the task. Translating demanded an ever-extending range of language for the more competent speakers (a searching and range which would provide some very useful ways into literary criticism).

(4) Some children (only a few) felt somewhat removed from the oral culture. They clearly identified with the English translations of stories they saw in books, and wished to have access to them and make them their own. One boy, who has clearly had a lot of negative experience in primary school, opted out by diligently copying out The three little pigs at home. Others clearly needed to regenerate their remembering of stories by consulting parents. There is a need to remember that some children are cut off both from the mother-tongue cultural tradition and those which are part of the cultural luggage of native English speakers.

(5) Not all stories which were told, shared and enjoyed were written up. The written work was usually divided between writing an English version, a mother-tongue version, and, for beginners, writing titles, etc.

One very small boy began a story in stanza form, very clearly a traditional opening. This — even though he could not finish it — earned him very high status in the group.

The larger framework

The project represents an attempt to place the second language learners in a context in which their mother tongue is a <u>positive</u> attribute — and not, as is usual, in a context in which this is a negative factor.

It attempts to open up the question of how schools can, through their existing departments and structures (e.g. art, drama, English, integrated studies, religous studies), begin to take on other cultures and use this as a <u>positive</u> factor in the curriculum.

There are, of course, problems which need to be very fully looked at. Clearly, subject teachers could not take this on without support of the the right kind. Equally, some of the stories are sexist (I think at least four women got burned alive). This element, along with the sex roles portrayed in Snow White, etc, would need to be talked through within the context of a whole-school policy on this issue.

It seems to me that we cannot begin to speak of multicultural education until we have thought out how we are to take on, recognise, respect and celebrate the culture of all kids — for our culture is something which seems so deep as to be a part of us.

A secondary school for girls reported:

(1) We have Urdu, Hindi and Punjabi classes to 'O' level, funded by the County Council;

(2) We enter pupils for mother-tongue 'O' levels and 'A' levels. The County Council pays the fees;

(3) We draw on mother-tongue skills in English projects — also have interesting work in religious education, art and music. Recently, we co-operated with a local university in a project to teach awareness, appreciation and composing techniques in Indian music.

(4) The library is multicultural and is using an integrated cataloguing system.

GROWING UP BILIN‹

All of these young people are growing up bilingu‹ probably reminds you of someone you teach.

Satnam is eighteen. He came to Britain, from India, with his family when he was seven years old. While he was at Junior school, he used to attend a voluntary Punjabi class two nights a week. He listened to some stories and began to learn to read Punjabi. When he went to Secondary school, however, he lost interest, and stopped going to the Punjabi lessons. Now Satnam is older and about to leave school, he has decided that he would like to know more about his parents' and his grandparents' country. He wants to learn how to read Punjabi but he is now too old to go to the voluntary classes.

Most Adult Education Institutes will organise a class and employ a teacher if there are eight or ten students interested in attending. Have you had any experience of helping a student in Satnam's situation get in touch with an AEI? Or of organising mother-tongue classes in AEIs or Colleges of Further Education?

If so, **NCLE** would like to hear from you.

Malik is eight years old. He speaks and reads English at home and at school. He also speaks Bengali at home, especially when he is with his grandfather. Malik's mother buys a Bengali newspaper every week, and he sometimes tries to read bits of it. But he has no simple story books to get his teeth into. So he is making slow progress in learning to read his mother-tongue language.

Are there children like Malik in your class? Have you managed to get hold of some picture books or story books that would help them get started with reading their mother tongues? Can your school library help? Have you worked out a way of involving parents, local minority language bookshops or the local library? Is your school successful in encouraging children to read and take home books in their mother-tongue languages?

If so **NCLE** would like to hear from you.

The Mother Tongue Sub-Committee of the **National Congress for Languages in Educatic** (NCLE) was set up in June 1980. One of its aim‹ is to discover, and document, the range of positi‹ responses which many schools across the count‹ have made to the multi-lingual nature of the

JAL

1e of them

Ana-Christine is fourteen. She has been in Britain for three years and is still learning to read and write English. School leaving exams are two years away, but her teachers do not expect her to pass in many subjects.

Ana-Christine can read and write Portuguese, but unfortunately this does not help her with her subject lessons. In two years time her English may be good enough for her to tackle the translation exercises which are part of the Portuguese 'O' level examination. But, unfortunately, her school does not enter bilingual students for 'O' levels in their mother-tongue languages.

Have you experience of using students' first language skills in order to help them master the content of mainstream subject lessons such as Maths, Science, Geography? Perhaps by providing a text book in an appropriate language, or a range of mother-tongue encyclopaedias in the school library, or, simply, a selection of translation dictionaries? Does your school enter bilingual students for 'O' levels in their mother-tongue languages. Are you able to organise some tuition or coaching (on however limited a scale) for these students? Are you able to draw on the mother tongue skills of bilingual students for the benefit of all the children in your class e.g. when you plan projects on 'Language', 'Community newspapers', etc?

If so, **NCLE** would like to hear from you.

Tin Wo is five years old. He speaks and under-stands Cantonese very well for his age. He doesn't yet understand very much English. He has just started school; a traumatic experience for all children. But it was worse for Tin Wo. He was completely isolated. No one in the school had worked out how to use Cantonese to communicate with him: to comfort him, to say what was expected of him, to help him find his way round school.

Has your school or nursery worked out ways of using children's mother-tongues to help them feel more at home during the first few weeks in the reception class? Perhaps by using parents, helpers or older children in the school? Have you thought of ways of using the different mother-tongues of your children as a source of pleasure and learning? Perhaps by getting children to teach each other their own songs and nursery rhymes. Or by getting a parent to come in and tell stories for everyone?

If so, **NCLE** would like to hear from you.

mmunities they serve. However tentative you
ıy feel about the work that's been done in **your**
ʰool or nursery, we would like to hear about it.
ᵉentually we hope to produce a report, which will
 widely circulated, and which will help us all to
ırn from one another's experience.

Please Contact

In addition to being sent the reports of work being done in schools represented above, the Working Party received two useful booklets, which it felt were particularly useful:

Talking and telling, produced by members of the Language Support Services in Berkshire. Two articles, in particular, are worth reading: 'Snake stories' and 'Mother tongue: the importance of Asian languages in Britain' (both written by teachers). Available from: The English Language Centre and Support Service, Lyndford Road, Reading; and Thomas Gray Language Centre, Queens Road, Slough.

Mother tongue: politics and practice, produced by Issues in Race and Education. Contains a practical/resource section which explores a range of reasons for introducing mother-tongue languages into the classroom (as an input medium; to stimulate work in English; to practice and develop the skills of interpretation and translation; to stimulate work for the whole class) and attempts to exemplify different kinds of work which can be done at infant reception, junior school, secondary and FE level. Available from: Issues in Race and Education, 11 Carleton Gardens, Brecknock Road, London N19 5AQ.

SELECT ANNOTATED BIBLIOGRAPHY

June Geach
Linguistic Minorities Information Officer, CILT

Entries in the bibliography relate primarily, but not exclusively, to the British situation and experience, and have been chosen from material easily accessible, for the most part, in Britain. Where relevant, items appear in more than one section, but a full citation is given once only.

    (A) General issues
    (B) Surveys, reviews, reports
    (C) Policy statements
    (D) Bilingual education
    (E) Bilingualism among minority groups in Britain

(A) General Issues

1. Commission for Racial Equality
Mother Tongue Teaching Conference report (Bradford College, September 1980); sponsored by the CRE and Bradford College. London: CRE; Bradford: Bradford College (1981).

Includes an analysis of mother tongue and mother-tongue teaching, a description of the attitude of the European Communities to mother-tongue teaching and a review of research, together with reports from the workshops on educational questions relating to pre-school, primary- and secondary-aged children.

2. Garner, M, ed
Community languages: their role in education. Melbourne/Sydney: River Seine Publications, 1981.

Covers theoretical issues (e.g. multiculturalism, language policy, bilingualism and bilingual education, community languages in schools), and reports on some actual experiences of community language programmes in Australia and elsewhere.

3. Hawkins, E
Modern languages in the curriculum. Cambridge: Cambridge University Press, 1981.

In the context of language awareness in the curriculum, puts forward a framework which could accommodate some study of minority ethnic languages.

4. Lewis, E Glyn
   Bilingualism and bilingual education. Oxford: Pergamon Press,
   1981.

   Wide-ranging treatment of the theoretical framework, with case
   studies from the Soviet Union, United States and Celtic Britain.

5. Little, A and R Willey
   Multi-ethnic education: the way forward. London: Schools
   Council, 1981. (Schools Council Pamphlet 18.)

   Surveys current provision in local education authorities and
   secondary schools and outlines priority areas for action in curriculum development, materials production and teacher training.

6. Marland, M
   Non-European languages and the curriculum. London: North
   Westminster Community School (ILEA), 1980. Discussion document
   for a symposium (December 1980).

   Sets forth criteria for the introduction of 'non-European' languages into the school curriculum for all pupils, both English
   mother-tongue speakers and speakers of mother tongues other than
   English, and suggests possible patterns of provision.

7. Saifullah Khan, V
   Bilingualism and linguistic minorities in Britain: developments,
   perspectives. London: Runnymede Trust, 1977.

   Reviews the thinking in Britain on mother-tongue maintenance and
   bilingual education and makes recommendations for promoting and
   maintaining bilingualism as a national resource.

8. Schools Council
   Examining in a multi-cultural society: the report of a confer-
   ence held at the Schools Council, September 1981. London:
   Schools Council, December 1981.

   Report of a conference convened to consider the implications and
   recommendations of the report Multi-ethnic education: the way
   forward (see 5 above) and the Rampton Committee of Enquiry
   Interim Report West Indian children in our schools. Covers
   general curriculum issues as well as subject-specific issues.
   Guidelines for development of examinations and a list of
   examinations already developed are set out in appendices.

9. Skutnabb-Kangas, T
    Guest worker or immigrant – different ways of reproducing an
    underclass. Journal of Multilingual and Multicultural Develop-
    ment, vol 2 no. 2, 1981, p89–115. Bibliography.

    An analysis of the effects of different types of educational
    provision for the children of, respectively, guest workers and
    immigrants; political and economic focus.

10. Tosi, A
    Immigration and bilingual education. Pergamon Press, to be pub-
    lished.

    To examine the notions of ethnic bilingualism and children's
    bilingualism. Special reference to mother tongue maintenance
    and methods of language transfer (natural and guided); case
    study of bilingualism among Italians in Bedford.

11. Wilding, C
    Languages, education and industry: a summary of reports and
    conferences prepared for the Research Committee on Foreign
    Languages in Industry and Commerce in the West Midlands.
    Birmingham: Department of Modern Languages, University of Aston
    in Birmingham, March 1980.

    Analyses reports on the language needs of industry, in some of
    which attention is drawn to specific need for knowledge of
    certain less commonly taught languages, including Portuguese,
    Arabic, Swedish, Japanese, Chinese. Description and evaluation
    of each conference and its recommendations; some consideration
    of the value of foreign languages in industry.

12. World yearbook of education 1981: Education of minorities;
    edited by J Megarry, S Nisbet and E Hoyle. London: Kogan Page;
    New York: Nichols Publishing Company, 1981.

    Discussion of problems from linguistic, psychological, socio-
    logical and cultural viewpoints. Bilingual education, factors
    underlying success or failure for pupils from a linguistic or
    cultural minority, home-school conflict, pressure on school
    provision are among the subjects treated. Extensive bibliog-
    raphy, with annotations of some important references.

(B) Surveys, reviews, reports

1. Mitchell, R
   <u>Bilingual education of minority language groups in the English-speaking world: some research evidence</u>. Stirling: Department of Education, University of Stirling, 1978. (Seminar Papers 4.)

   A survey of the research evidence on the achievement of minority groups in monolingual and bilingual formal education in the English-speaking world. Discusses the potentialities and limitations of native language medium education for individual speakers of minority languages and for the survival prospects of minority language communities.

2. Swain, M and J Cummins
   Bilingualism, cognitive functioning and education. Survey article. <u>Language Teaching & Linguistics: Abstracts</u>, vol 12 no. 1, 1979.

   Reviews studies which have investigated the relationship between bilingual and cognitive functioning, and outlines the implications of these research findings for educational settings.

3. Tosi, A
   Mother-tongue teaching for the children of migrants. Survey article. <u>Language Teaching & Linguistics: Abstracts</u>, vol 12 no. 4, October 1979. (Also available as an offprint from the National Council for Mother-Tongue Teaching.)

   Surveys studies on the philosophy, objectives and implications of bilingual education, and outlines their relevance in the context of the migration of workers in Europe. Bibliography.

4. Tosi, A
   Issues in im/migrant bilingualism, 'semilingualism' and education. <u>AILA</u> (Association Internationale de Linguistique Appliquée) <u>Bulletin</u>, no. 2(31), January 1982.

   A review of studies since the author's survey article (<u>see</u> 3 <u>above</u>) on language education for linguistically diverse children in America and Europe. Emphasis on material directly relevant to linguistic conditions of im/migrant children.

(C) Policy statements

1. Centre for Information on Language Teaching and Research
   Comments on the report and recommendations of the Committee of
   Inquiry on the Education of Children from Ethnic Minority Groups
   (Interim Report): <u>West Indian children in our schools</u>) and the
   Fifth Report from the Home Affairs Committee of the House of
   Commons. London: CILT, December 1981.

   Recommendations on teaching English as a second language, the
   multicultural curriculum for languages, teacher training and
   funding, in response to the consultative document circulated by
   the Department of Education and Science.

2. Commission for Racial Equality
   <u>The EEC's Directive on the education of children of migrant
   workers: its implications for the education of children from
   ethnic minority groups in the UK.</u> London: CRE, October 1980.

   The Commission's interpretation of the provisions of the Directive (<u>see</u> 3 <u>below</u>), and their effect in a British context.

3. Commission for Racial Equality
   <u>Ethnic minority community languages:</u> a statement. London: CRE,
   August 1982.

   A policy statement supporting the maintenance of language
   diversity as an asset in a multi-cultural society, through a
   programme of mother-tongue teaching throughout the formal
   education system from infant to higher education. Among the
   major issues considered are teacher training, development of
   examinations in languages as mother tongues, bilingualism and
   bilingual education, desirable policy in central and local
   government.

4. Council of the European Economic Community
   <u>On the education of the children of migrant workers:</u> Council
   Directive of 25 July 1977. Brussels: EEC, 1977. (777/486/EEC.)

   Instructs member states of the European Communities to take
   appropriate measures to promote the teaching of the mother
   tongue and of the culture of the country of origin of the children of migrant workers, and also, as part of compulsory free
   education, to teach one or more of the official languages of the
   host state; the measures necessary to comply with the Directive
   to be instituted within four years of notification of the
   Directive.

5. Department of Education and Science/Welsh Office Joint circular
    no. 5/81 (DES)/no. 36/81(Welsh Office)
    <u>Directive of the Council of the European Community on the educa-</u>
    <u>tion of the children of migrant workers.</u> London/Cardiff, July
    1981.

    The requirements of the Directive (<u>see</u> 3 <u>above</u>), in the view of
    the Department, and measures taken to comply with it.

6. Department of Education and Science/Welsh Office
    <u>A framework for the school curriculum</u>: proposals for consulta-
    tion by the Secretaries of State for Education and Science and
    for Wales. London: DES/Welsh Office, January 1980.

    Presents a view of the aims of the curriculum and of local edu-
    cation authority responsibility within which LEAs could justify
    support, in British terms, for mother tongues other than
    English.

7. Department of Education and Science/Welsh Office
    <u>The school curriculum</u>. London: Her Majesty's Stationery Office,
    March 1981.

    Refers, in the section on modern languages, to the valuable
    individual and national resource provided by pupils whose first
    language is not English or Welsh, and the Secretaries of State
    undertake to further the work required on modern languages.

8. National Association for Multiracial Education
    <u>Mother tongue and minority community languages in education.</u>
    Policy paper. Derby: NAME, 1981.

    States the case for putting community/home languages into the
    curriculum, on a par with the more commonly taught European
    languages, and considers some associated matters: e.g. recruit-
    ment of teachers, development of teaching materials, development
    of examinations.

9. National Council for Mother-Tongue Teaching
    Submission on the fifth report of the Home Affairs Committee of
    the House of Commons (<u>Racial disadvantage</u>, 1981). London: NCMTT,
    1981.

    A response to the consultative document circulated by the
    Department of Education and Science; comments in particular on
    minority languages in schools, teacher education, collection of
    statistics, funding.

10. National Union of Teachers
    <u>Linguistic diversity and mother tongue teaching</u>. Policy statement. London: NUT, 1982.

    Calls for the same status to be accorded to ethnic minority languages as to other modern European languages in the schools, and urges the DES to give a clear lead to local education authorities on the implementation of practical strategies for increasing the level of mother-tongue teaching in schools wherever it is appropriate. Promises the full support of the Union for this and for the implementation of procedures to enable teachers with overseas certification to gain qualified teacher status in Britain.

11. Scottish Education Department
    <u>Directive of the Council of the European Community on the education of the children of migrant workers</u>. Circular 1071. Edinburgh: SED, August 1981.

    The Department's view of the Directive, with guidance to education authorities on ways of complying with it; special reference to provision for teaching English as a second language and to possible ways of supporting the mother tongues of minority communities.

(D) Bilingual education

1. Baetens Beardsmore, H
    <u>Bilingualism</u>: basic principles. Clevedon, Avon: Tieto Ltd, 1982.

    A study of bilingualism in the individual; themes and definitions, interference and code-switching, measurement of bilingualism, problems of bilingual speakers, surveys of literature and research in the field. Extensive bibliography.

2. Centre for Information on Language Teaching and Research
    <u>Bilingualism and British education: the dimensions of diversity</u>. London: CILT, 1976. (CILT Reports and Papers 14.)

    Papers from a conference which considered the problems of bilingual children whose mother tongues are largely ignored educationally; examples of planned or structured bilingual education in Wales, and the relationship between the techniques of foreign language teaching and the notion and reality of bilingualism.

3. Cummins, J
   <u>Bilingualism and minority-language children</u>. Toronto, Ontario:
   OISE (Ontario Institute for Studies in Education) Press, 1981.
   (Language and Literacy Series.)

   Reviews research findings and theories related to bilingualism
   in children whose first or home language is different from the
   language of the wider community and its schools. Focus on Canadian context, but the principles of bilingualism and bilingual
   education considered are applicable in other national contexts.

4. Fishman. J A
   <u>Bilingual education: an international sociological perspective</u>.
   Rowley, Massachusetts: Newbury House Publishers, 1976.

   A sociological approach to bilingual education addressed primarily to teachers, teacher-trainees, educational administrators
   and other specialists, but also for the interested layman.

5. Skutnabb - Kangas, Tove
   <u>Bilingualism or not: the education of minorities</u>, Clevedon,
   Avon: Multilingual Matters, 1983.

   A thorough treatment of the phenomenon of bilingualism, and
   associated educational research issues. Very full bibliography.

6. Swain, M
   <u>Bilingual education for majority and minority language children</u>.
   Plenary paper presented at conference of AILA (Association
   Internationale de Linguistique Appliquée), Lund, Sweden, August
   1981. Published in <u>Studia Linguistica</u>, vol 35, no. 1 - 2, 1981,
   p 15-32.

   Description of the Canadian French programme and analysis of the
   significance of its results; puts the case for the importance of
   sequencing of the languages of instruction in the development of
   bilingual proficiency within an educational system.
   Bibliography.

   Swain and Cummins: see B2.

(E) Bilingualism among minority groups in Britain

1. Brook, M R M
   The 'mother-tongue' issue in Britain: cultural diversity or control? British Journal of Sociology of Education, vol 1 no. 3, 1980, p 237-55.

   Discusses critically the history, scope and purposes of the Directive of the Council of the European Communities on the education of the children of migrant workers (see C3) and examines its significance for language policies in Britain. Particular consideration given to the term 'mother tongue'. (A revised and edited version of this paper is available from M R Brook, Faculty of Education, King's College, London.)

2. Campbell-Platt, K
   Linguistic minorities in Britain. Briefing paper. Revised by S Nicholas. London: Runnymede Trust, August 1978.

   A statistical survey of the main overseas-born minorities in Britain which maintain their mother tongue, and the distribution in Britain of populations born in selected countries in Europe, Africa, Asia and Oceania and the West Indies.

3. Derrick, J
   Language needs of minority group children: learners of English as a second language. Windsor: NFER Publishing Co, 1977.

   Reviews aspects of teaching English as a second language; special reference to issues in bilingualism, linguistic and cultural identity.

4. European Communities Bedfordshire Mother Tongue Culture Pilot Project; report of a colloquium held at Cranfield Institute of Technology, March 1980. Rapporteurs R Bourne and J Trim.

   Provides a chronological account of the proceedings (R Bourne) and an analytical account of the issues which arose (J Trim). (May be consulted at the Language Teaching Library, 20 Carlton House Terrace, London SW1Y 5AP.)

5. Le Page, R B
   Caribbean connections in the classroom. London: Mary Glasgow Language Trust, 1981.

   A pamphlet of guidance for teachers concerned with the language problems of children of Afro-Caribbean descent. Includes notes on the history of West Indian Creoles, samples of Creole texts, and suggestions for the teacher's approach to the use of Creole and English in the classroom. Sociolinguistic approach.

6. Russell, R
   Ethnic minority languages and the schools (with special reference to Urdu). London: Runnymede Trust, 1980.

   Considers the problems of organisation, syllabus development,
   and provision of teaching materials involved in providing mother
   tongue teaching in schools, and makes suggestions on teaching
   methodology and materials (for Urdu).

7. Saifullah Khan, V
   The 'mother-tongue' of linguistic minorities in multicultural
   England. Journal of Multilingual and Multicultural Development,
   vol 1 no. 1, 1980, p 71-88.

   A general introduction to bilingualism and mother-tongue teaching which is confined to the situation in England. History and
   current situation, main components in the provision of mother-
   tongue teaching, significant economic, political and social
   factors in ethnic relations.

8. Wilding, J
   Ethnic minority languages in the classroom?: a survey of Asian
   parents in Leicester. Leicester: Leicester Council for Community Relations and Leicester City Council, November 1981.

   The author generalises from the results of a survey of Gujara-
   ti-, Punjabi- or Kutchi-speaking parents to determine the extent
   of parental support for maintaining these languages for their
   children and demand for facilities in teaching them. Useful
   brief survey of publications and other major research projects
   in Britain.

9. Wright, J
   Bilingualism in education. London: Centre for Urban Educational
   Studies, 1980. (Occasional Paper 1.)

   Reviews theories of bilingualism, some research findings and
   programmes of bilingual education outside Britain, and suggests
   ways in which such programmes might develop in Britain.

RECENT AND CURRENT RESEARCH PROJECTS IN ENGLAND CILT RESEARCH REGISTER

This is a list of some major research projects concerned with the relationship between 'minority' languages and education in Britain. The numbers at the end of each description refer to the entry in the research register maintained at CILT; fuller information may be obtained by consulting the register. Main published results, where known, are listed for each project.

EEC/Bedfordshire Pilot Project: Mother tongue and culture 1976-1980:

The project was designed to investigate the educational implications for Italian- and Punjabi-speaking children of providing some education in their mother tongue and culture in five Bedford schools, and to assess the effect on non-participating pupils. Part of the European Communities' education programme. (Enquiries and correspondence to D P J Browning, Bedfordshire County Council, County Hall, Bedford MK42 9AP.) 2030.

'Mother tongue and culture' in Bedfordshire: EEC-sponsored pilot project. External evaluation reports. Cambridge: Cambridge Institute of Education, 1979-80.

First evaluation (January 1978-September 1978): details the setting up of the project and the initial experience of those involved.

Second evaluation (September 1978 – September 1979): explores some of the central issues in mother-tongue, multi-cultural and bilingual education, primarily through the perspectives of participants in the project.

An unpublished report of the Colloquium held in April 1980 on completion of the project may be consulted at CILT.

Bilingual Education Project (Inner London Education Authority) 1977-1980

The project aimed to produce bilingual materials for use in secondary schools, to enable children who can read in their mother tongue (a language other than English) to have access to some of their learning materials in various curriculum subjects in their mother tongue. (Director: J Wright; Project was based at the Centre for Urban Educational Studies, London.) 2238.

The World in a city (materials in 8 languages: Chinese, Greek, Spanish, Turkish, Bengali, Gujarati, Punjabi, Urdu). London: ILEA Learning Materials Service, 1982. Distributed by the Commission for Racial Equality, London.

Linguistic Minorities Project (1979–83)

The overall aim of this project, funded by the Department of Education and Science, is to provide an account and analysis of the changing patterns of bilingualism in several regions of England, and incidentally to develop and assess varied methodologies for the study of the processes of language change and shift. Surveys are being carried out of the range of linguistic diversity in all schools in a number of local education authorities, the perceptions and use of language of secondary school pupils in some of the areas, and language use by adults. Information is also being collated on all forms of mother tongue provision in a few areas. (Director: Dr V Saifullah Khan; Project base: University of London Institute of Education, 18 Woburn Square, London WC1H ONS.) See also Mother Tongue Teaching Directory below. 2361.

Couillaud, X, V Saifullah Khan and E Reid: Summary of the Mother Tongue Teaching Directory survey findings in Bradford, Coventry and Haringey. 1983.

Linguistic Minorities Project: England's other languages. (Provisional title.) London: Routledge & Kegan Paul, forthcoming 1984.

The Schools Language Survey: summary of findings from five LEAs. Language Information Network Coordination, May 1983.

Linguistic minorities in England: a short report on the Linguistic Minorities Project. September 1983.

Linguistic minorities in England: a report for the Department of Education and Science. London: University of London, Institute of Education, December 1983. Distributed by Tinga Tinga (Heinemann Educational Books Ltd, Redhill, Surrey)

Reports and papers obtainable from address below: Information Office, University of London, Institute of Education, 20 Bedford Way, London WC1 OAL.

Mother Tongue and English Teaching Project (MOTET) (1978-1980)

A DES-sponsored project which explored the effect on young Punjabi-speaking children of different kinds of usage of their two languages in their school career; half the reception class curriculum for a school year was taught through the medium of Punjabi, half through English, and a matched group of children was taught entirely through English in the conventional pattern, the effects being monitored in detail. Completed 1980. (Directors: Dr O A Rees, Postgraduate School of Studies in Research Education, University of Bradford and F Fitzpatrick, Bradford College.) 2346.

MOTET: summary of the report; vols 1 and 2. Bradford, 1981.

Mother Tongue Teaching Directory

Developed by the National Council for Mother-Tongue Teaching in collaboration with the Linguistic Minorities Project as a standardised means of documenting the range and type of teaching of minority languages in different areas of England. Aims to provide information about the numbers of pupils learning minority languages and the situation faced by pupils, teachers and organisers in the voluntary sector and in maintained schools. Regular up-dating envisaged; administration by NCMTT. (Enquiries to R Truman, NCMTT, 5 Musgrave Crescent, London SW6 4PT.)

Schools Council Mother Tongue Project (1981-)

Aims to produce exemplar teaching materials in Greek and Bengali which may be useful as guides to producing materials in other minority languages, and to produce handbooks and guides for bilingual teachers and for monolingual teachers wishing to support their pupils' bilingualism. (Director: D Houlton; Project base: Centre for Urban Educational Studies, Robert Montefiore School, Underwood Road, London E1 5AD.) 2772.

Termly Newsletter to give information on progress of the project, and to offer and maintain an information exchange with interested persons outside the project.

SUMMARY DISCUSSION DOCUMENT AND RECOMMENDATIONS FROM THE WORKING PARTY

(A) Principles

At present the teaching of the languages of minority communities takes place in Britain largely through voluntary effort, outside the formal school sector. There are three basic types of justification for an increased contribution from the official school system to what we will refer to in this document as Community Language Teaching - CLT.

(1) For the individual child CLT provides a link between home and school, supports the development of an extended competence in more than one language rather than perhaps allowing early skills in a language other than English simply to wither away, and contributes to the development of a secure personal identity.

(2) For the minority language communities CLT in schools can enhance their sometimes marginal position in the education system by making it clear that their languages are fully valued by the mainstream.

(3) For all pupils and students CLT can increase awareness, knowledge and understanding regarding minority communities, and Contribute to the development of a genuinely multi-cultural curriculum.

In areas of Britain where sufficient numbers of children speaking particular community languages other than English are to be found in schools, and where substantial local community demand can be shown to exist, as part of the normal process of responding to local conditions, the education system ought to respond by making provision for CLT.

(B) Priorities

We suggest the following as the points where the education system should first develop its contribution:

(1) In the use of community languages in the initial school reception of young children speaking such a language before school entry.

(2) In the development for such potentially bilingual children of literacy in the community language as well as in English.

(3) In the establishment of community languages as school subjects certificated on the same basis as other modern languages.

(C) Detailed Recommendations

For implementation at <u>Local Level</u> by LEAs and Schools.

1. On the basis of up-to-date information regarding the numbers and distribution of children in their area having languages other than English as a mother tongue (available for example from the Schools Language Surveys designed by the Linguistic Minorities Project), and on the basis of consultation with minority language communities to establish local demand, LEAs should develop an explicit CLT policy appropriate to local circumstances. Such a policy should include the identification of a limited number of local languages on which available resources would in the first place be concentrated.

2. With reference to each of the languages identified in such a policy, advice should be sought from all interested parties about the scope and objectives of CLT syllabuses, as well as about the division of responsibility for CLT between voluntary and maintained sectors.

3. A staffing policy should be adopted within the LEA with the object of including at least one speaker of each of the identified languages among the permanent staff of relevant schools. School-based and/or peripatetic teachers, as well as auxiliaries and community helpers, should be allocated to meet the level of CLT provision locally felt appropriate.

4. Through its Teachers' Centres and Advisory Service the LEA should also provide facilities for inservice training, local materials production, and communication between different local groups working in CLT and in other types of language teaching.

5. For each locally identified language, LEAs should provide places for children in nursery and reception classes which have bilingual staff; in such classes, alongside systematic instruction in English as a second language, learning would also continue through the medium of the home language.

6. It should be the objective for CLT to children of primary age that all children speaking one of the locally identified languages would have the opportunity to become literate in that language. To this end systematic instruction should be provided for such children in literacy skills, for a specified number of hours per week, whether by their class teacher, another teacher in the school, or a peripatetic teacher.

7. At secondary school level, speakers of locally identified languages should have the opportunity to pursue studies of these languages to an advanced level, and LEAs should ensure that as part of any language diversification policy that sufficient schools in their area were offering courses in them.

8. Some community languages should be available to all children whether or not they have family connection with the language, on a similar basis to other modern languages, and as an addition to the range of languages generally on offer in the schools.

9. Special attention should be given to the development of learning methods appropriate to very mixed levels of previous experience of a language, so that an at least partial integration of 'native speakers' and other learners may be made possible; self-access approaches should be considered in this context.

10. School records should normally include information on languages used at home, and on parents' views about which languages should be fostered at school; and school prospectuses should as a matter of course include details of CLT facilities offered.

11. LEAs should offer tangible assistance to local language teachers to extend their own knowledge of community languages.

12. Since the development of CLT within the maintained sector will involve many organisaional and methodological innovations, LEAs and schools should begin immediately by mounting pilot projects with particular languages and at different stages of schooling, building on existing experience, as a foundation for the implementation of larger-scale programmes.

For implementation at National Level.

13. To provide a national focus for the allsided development of CLT in both maintained and voluntary sectors, we propose the establishment of a number of Language Development & Training Units, in the first place for the most widely-used languages of minority communities in Britain. Their functions would include the preparation of syllabuses, development of methodologies, materials, examinations, in-service and initial teacher training, and related research.

14. We recommend that there should also be a single national 'clearing-house' for the exchange of information regarding all aspects of CLT, including the progress of the pilot projects referred to in 12 above.

15. A long-term planned approach to the provision of public examinations in community languages is an essential element in the promotion of CLT on a national basis. Between them the various examination boards and groupings should ensure the availability of a full range of examinations at each level. New developments in the form of assessment and certification ought also to take account of these languages, and we recommend that the skills in all the languages with which an individual is acquainted should be recorded in a profile prepared in the final year of schooling.

16. Opportunities for study at degree and postgraduate level of languages which are important to the minority communities in Britain and for teacher training in these languages should be safeguarded and developed on a planned national basis, with particular reference to the staffing needs implied by our recommendations.

* This document was prepared originally to help focus discussion of the Working Party's Report and Supporting Papers at the July 1982 NCLE Assembly in Nottingham.

CILT

**Centre for Information on
Language Teaching and Research**

provides

Modern Language Teachers

with

INFORMATION

on all aspects of modern language teaching - materials
methodology and research.

****

To: CILT, 20 Carlton House Terrace, London SW1Y

Please send me details of your information services and
publications.

NAME..

SCHOOL..

ADDRESS...

....